"This isn't macabre stuff; it's funny and poignant and, as you dig in, it's very, very addicting. Once you've started *Over Our Dead Bodies*, in fact, you'll like it to The End." —TERRI SCHLICHENMEYER ("The Bookworm")

"These tales are not only true and real, but funny and amusing. This book is, in a word, fun. I enjoyed every story in this very lively book."
—*Hudson Valley News*

"Ken McKenzie has made a name for himself, not just as a funeral director but as a public advocate for the industry. In his new book he shows readers that undertaking can be a lot more fun than it sounds. *Over Our Dead Bodies* is a morbidly humorous personal account of McKenzie's career in the funeral business." —*Signal Tribune*

"Outrageous funeral stories, dipped in beauty and morbid humor . . . As a sixth-generation funeral director, my family has a bunch of stories we like to tell, but *none* like this one. I recommend this book as a well-written peek into the funeral industry. If you're looking for a fun book to read on vacation; or a weird Christmas gift to give to your macabre Uncle Frank; or maybe you're interested in what funeral directors might encounter; or you simply want to support Ken's KAMM Cares, let me recommend *Over Our Dead Bodies*."
—CALEB WILDE, author of *Confessions of a Funeral Director*

"A lively collection of behind the scenes at the funeral home stories—moving stories of unexpected send-offs, family feuds in the funeral home, and disasters that happen to the people who work to make funerals run smoothly. A fun read that provides a personal glimpse into the funeral business." —GAIL RUBIN, author of *A Long Goodbye*

"We're treated to the kind of tales we'd normally beg to hear when we'd meet an undertaker at a cocktail party." —*The Director*

Books by
KENNETH MCKENZIE and TODD HARRA

Mortuary Confidential

Over Our Dead Bodies

Available from Citadel Press,
an imprint of Kensington Publishing Corp.

Over Our Dead Bodies

UNDERTAKERS LIFT THE LID

Kenneth McKenzie

AND

Todd Harra

Citadel Press
KENSINGTON PUBLISHING CORP.
WWW.KENSINGTONBOOKS.COM

CITADEL PRESS BOOKS are published by

Kensington Publishing Corp.
119 West 40th Street New
York, NY 10018

All Kensington titles, imprints, and distributed lines are available at special
quantity dscounts for bulk purchases for sales promotions, premiums, fund-raising,
educational, or institutional use. Special book excerpts or customized printings can
also be created to fit specific needs. For details, write or phone the office of the
Kensington sales manager: Kensington Publishing Corp., 119 West 40th Street,
New York, NY 10018, attn: Sales Department; phone 1-800-221-2647.

First trade paperback printing: June 2014

ISBN: 978-0-8065-4141-9

Printed in the United States of America

10 9 8 7 6 5 4 3 2

Electronic edition:

ISBN: 978-0-8065-3665-1 (e-book)

For Rick, who taught me the trade.

Order of Service

I am able to say that while I am not so ruggedly well, I am not ill enough to excite an undertaker.

—MARK TWAIN

CHAPTER 1

There's No Such Thing as a Normal Day

E ven though I knew it was coming, it was still a shock— as it's supposed to be—as my front doors crashed back on their hinges and policemen flooded in. I found myself staring into the business end of a lot of pistols and I think a shotgun or two. I don't really remember. When there are guns pointed at me my mind tends to go to mush.

"Against the wall!" a voice behind one of the pistols commanded.

And though my mind was shouting *I'm the owner! I'm the owner!* I merely stumbled up against the wall as the wave swept past me, less one officer, who gave me a pat down.

From the parking lot, I could hear the screams of a man overshadowed by an officer yelling, "Stop resisting! Stop resisting!"

In retrospect, the day hadn't started out so bad, and if I had known it would have ended with BioTech—a crime scene remediation service—scrubbing blood out of the carpet and off the walls, I never would've gotten out of bed that morning. No funeral is worth that kind of aggravation, not to mention being frisked like a teenage girl on prom night.

It was a Saturday, deceptively sunny and warm for what grief the day would bring. I arrived at my place, McKenzie Mortuary, located in Belmont Heights, Long Beach, early, made coffee and took messages off the answering service, and then took Ruthless, my goldendoodle, for a walk around the block before locking him in my office. My morning routine complete, I went into the chapel to get everything ready for the Revis service. I had dressed and casketed Mrs. Revis the day before, and sometime during the evening the hairdresser had come and done her hair and makeup. I checked the makeup and, satisfied, set about transferring all the flowers from the flower room to the chapel and setting them up around the casket.

Arranging floral tributes is a tricky art. We always set the family pieces closest to the deceased, the closer the degree of kinship, the closer to the casket, followed by coordinating colors and styles. Therefore, what might look best isn't necessarily what is set up because of how close or far from the casket the piece has to sit due to kinship. Mrs. Revis had a large family; I filled the entire front chapel wall around her casket with flowers.

I tinkered and fussed with all the floral arrangements and, finally satisfied, I set out the memorial folders and guest book in the lobby, and set up the Casio keyboard that one of the family members would play during the service at the front of the chapel. I spent the remaining time until the family arrived with a cloth and bottle of Windex shining up glass, mirrors, and furniture— nervous energy, really.

Mrs. Revis's son, Charles, and daughter, Jeanette, arrived shortly after 9 A.M. with their families, and went in and viewed their mother. As is my usual modus operandi, I waited a few minutes, heard some muffled weeping, and then swept into the room with a box of tissues. "Is everything all right . . . as far as her appearance is concerned?" I inquired.

Charles, tears in his eyes, replied, "She looks wonderful."

"Twenty years younger," Jeanette chimed in.

I beamed inwardly and simply nodded, "Good. If you need anything, I'll be in the lobby greeting your guests."

Charles took that opportunity to pull me aside. He had *that* look in his eye. "Look, Ken," he spoke in a whisper, "there's some . . . tension in the family."

"Oh?" I replied. There usually is. Combine the emotions surrounding the death of a family member with the impending estate settlement (i.e., money) and you can have a tense situation.

"Yeah, my two younger brothers didn't have much to do with my mother."

I nodded. I knew he had two brothers because they had been mentioned in the death notice.

"I don't know if they'll come or not. I hope they don't, but if they do they might cause trouble."

Oh great! I thought. I wished he had let me in on this little tidbit of knowledge days ago when we had made the arrangements. I have in the past hired off duty police officers to sit in for funerals where trouble was expected. Instead, I reassured him, "Don't worry. I deal with this all too frequently. I'm sure it'll be fine."

Famous last words: *It'll be fine.*

It wouldn't be.

It's amazing how calming the presence of a uniformed officer merely *sitting* in a lobby can be. In two instances, I have had them spring into action to prevent a disaster. But getting an off duty officer with no notice on a Saturday was out of the question. I'd have an easier time conjuring a genie from one of the urns in my showroom. I knew I'd just have to grin and bear it and hope.

As it turns out hope wasn't enough. Not by a long shot.

I knew them as soon as I laid eyes on them. They slunk in like two wolves, all easy strides and furtive glances behind Wayfarer shades they didn't take off, even in the dimness of the mortuary.

I extended the sleeve of my newly pressed suit to point at the guest book. "Sign the book, please."

Not a glance in my direction. They just glided by.

There they are, I thought, *the prodigal sons have arrived.* And I was correct. The wolves set up camp at the foot end of the casket, opposite Charles and Jeanette.

When a guest arrived they would greet either the camp at the head end of the casket or the foot end. Never both. There was a clear division in the family.

Thankfully, everyone behaved during the visitation, and if it was half as uncomfortable for them as it was for me witnessing it, then it was a pretty painful hour for the family members. I was glad to get all the guests seated and get the service started. My chapel has pew seating with a center aisle, and I was guessing by who sat on what side which camp they sided with.

I went into the deserted lobby and let out a sigh of relief. Everyone would behave during the service because it was structured. Whenever there has been a problem in the past it has been during the visitation. That is the unstructured part, when people can find ways to get into trouble. But people sit in silence and *listen* during a service and generally behave. I didn't know it, but this was going to be a first.

The service sailed along smoothly until it came time for people to offer testimony. This is when members of the audience get up and share thoughts and memories about the deceased. Each of the children, even the wolves, got up in turn and read a little something they had pre-written about their mother. It was very touching.

"Anyone else care to testify?" the considerably sized clergywoman asked.

A man in a three-piece suit sitting on the side of Charles and Jeanette stood up and walked up to the microphone. He identified himself as Earl, Mrs. Revis's brother. Without preamble, Earl started right in. "Ray and Sam," he said, pointing to the wolves, "You ought to be ashamed of yourselves." He jabbed a finger at them. "You treated your mother poorly. A God-fearing woman, she didn't deserve that. It's shameful, just shame—"

One of the wolf brothers stood up and yelled, "You'd wouldn't visit her either if she had cut you out of the will while your siblings stood by and took your share! Besides, who are you to stand and give judgment?"

Charles, red-faced, stood up and said loudly, "Maybe if you hadn't been stealing from her, she wouldn't have cut you off!"

A wolf, I wasn't sure which, stepped from his pew.

I was in the back, frantically motioning for the clergywoman to step in and take control by making a cutting motion across my throat.

"Stealing?" the wolf said. "Is that what you call it? Guess you didn't tell Earl what you—"

Charles cut him off, while advancing toward him, "Don't you say it, you no-good, thieving liar!"

They met at the center aisle, where the casket sat. I was running down the aisle yelling, "Stop!" when the wolf yelled, "You lousy sonofabitch!" as his fist connected with Charles's face. There was an audible, stomach-turning *crunch* as Charles's nose broke. I stopped as I saw an arc of blood spray across the interior cap panel (the inside portion of the lid) and Charles slump against the casket, pushing it into the wall with a loud *bam!* The force of the casket toppled several floral pieces.

It was totally silent for a second, and then the place erupted like a powder keg. It was like a fight out of an old Western. Men began leaping over pews and going at it, grabbing the giant marble pedestals from under the flower arrangements and throwing them. Even the women were setting into it, clawing and scratching and swinging their purses around.

I turned tail and ran to the lobby and grabbed the phone on the receptionist's desk and dialed.

"9-1-1, what's your emergency?" The voice on the line asked.

"I'm calling from McKenzie Mortuary, there's a"—I racked my brain for exactly what this situation was—"riot going on!"

"A fight?"

"No, many people fighting. A riot! Send police! Fast!"

I heard her say "Stay on the line" as I dropped the receiver and yelled at a man grabbing a big heavy brass sign that said SIGN GUEST BOOK, PLEASE.

"Hey!" I yelled.

The man with the sign ignored me.

Another man emerged from the chapel and the man armed with the sign took a mighty swing. Thankfully, the unarmed man ducked because the sign drove into the drywall with a *thud* and stuck. As the man tried to free the sign the man who ducked decked him, kicked over the guest book stand, and fled out the front door.

The man who had been the aggressor lay on the floor, blood leaking from his head. I started to venture over to him, but he suddenly sat up and shook his head as if to clear the cobwebs, and I jumped back behind the receptionist desk as if the faux-granite-laminate peninsula was some kind of substantial barrier.

The man freed the sign from the wall and ran into the melee in the chapel.

I should have stayed in my little safety zone behind the receptionist's desk, but I had a visceral urge to see what was happening. I ventured toward the chapel doors.

Several clients, who were making funeral arrangements, poked their heads out of one of the small offices. I could tell by the puzzled looks on their faces they weren't sure if they should be scared of the ruckus or not. I made a frantic motioning with my hands. "Get back! Get back!" I whisper-yelled. "Police are on the way." The puzzled faces quickly disappeared and the door closed.

As I approached the chapel, several people fled the scene, and each time I jumped over to the far wall as if to hide. Luckily, they were too intent on fleeing to bother me. Emboldened, I ducked into the rear of the chapel, and what I saw shocked me. The casket was toppled over and everything that wasn't bolted down had been tossed everywhere, ostensibly used as weapons. All my precious antiques were mostly shattered. Flower petals and blossoms poured from the sky like a ticker tape parade—the floral arrangements had been thrown and re-thrown and re-thrown. And of course the blood—it was everywhere. The walls. The carpets. The pews. I wanted to cry, but instead I shouted at the top of my lungs, "Police! The police are coming!"

Nobody paid a lick of attention to me, and then a wooden tissue box cover hit me in the face.

Really, it just grazed my jaw, but I was disoriented for a few moments. When I got my bearings, one of the rioters, a scrappy little guy with a ripped shirt, was screaming, "Police, police are here!"

The mob listened to him.

The place emptied out like somebody had fired a gun.

In mere seconds I was alone in the wreckage of my chapel. It was deathly silent compared to the screams and shouts of a few moments prior. I swooned, not from the minute pain in my jaw, but from the destruction done to my chapel.

I returned to the lobby to make sure the rioters had left the building and that's when I came face-to-face with the boys in blue and a couple of nasty-looking weapons.

They moved quickly through the building, a neat little train of shields and tactical gear. I heard "Police! Police! Open this door!" as they moved through the building, then frantic calling from behind the door: "Hold on! We have to move some furniture!"

There was muted scraping and thumping as furniture was moved and the door opened. The officers did a quick once over and, seeing there wasn't a threat, moved on through the building. I heard distant pounding followed by, "Police! Police! Open up!"

I winced when I heard the crunch of a splintering door jamb.

I was still being corralled against a lobby wall when the officers that had searched the building came back. The apparent team leader flipped the visor up on his helmet and reported to a man in sergeant's stripes who pushed his way into the lobby, "Nobody here, Sarge, but a few people in this office"—he motioned to the office where the people had barricaded themselves in—"and a terrified dog."

"No gun?"

"No."

The sergeant looked at me hard for a moment and then went and peeked into the chapel, then came back and asked the officer with the visor on his helmet, "Any other ways out?"

"Plenty. Could've gone out any of them; we just know he's not hiding in here. We searched every square inch."

Sarge turned his attention to me. "What's going on here?" he demanded.

"You tell me!" I said a bit too shrilly. "I called *you* because there's a riot going on in *my* building."

He inspected what I saw to be my wallet that had been taken from me during the search. He looked ay my ID, then me, then back at my ID. "You're Kenneth McKenzie," he finally said.

"Yes! That's what I was trying to tell you when you had the guns pointed at me."

He twitched his mustache and squinted at me hard before saying, "Let him go."

The officer guarding me stepped aside as if to tacitly acknowledge my newfound freedom.

Sarge flipped my wallet at me.

Of course I missed.

"Sorry about that, Mr. McKenzie." I wasn't sure if he was referring to having weapons pointed at me or the premature toss of my wallet. He was about to say something else when an officer stepped inside and whispered something in his ear. "Uh, Mr. McKenzie," Sarge said, seemingly embarrassed, "The members of the Revis family would like to know if they can view their mother one last time."

I bristled, but then remembered my professional obligation. "Fine," I said. "Your men can escort them in, " I said, shaking my finger at him, "one by one for a last look. And then you can tell them if they want any further information about their mother they can contact the medical examiner's office. I am turning their mother over to the state."

Minutes later, I stood in the lobby, holding a paper towel full of ice to my jaw, and glowered at the family members as they were escorted in in shackles. The officer escorting one of the wolves muttered to me on the way out, "They really did a number on your place."

Sarge later told me that as the first-responding officers arrived family members from the mob told them there were people in the building with guns. He thinks they tried using that as a ruse so they could slip away.

Their plan didn't succeed. The officers tased several of the more unruly funeral-goers in the parking lot. Hence, the screams I had heard.

All they found was me, some bereaved people hiding in an office with furniture piled in front of and door, an employee or two . . . and Ruthless, hiding under my desk.

Needless to say, I now boycott the phrase "It'll be fine" because I've learned the hard way that sometimes it won't be. No matter what you do or plan for, sometimes you find yourself literally (and figuratively) at gunpoint.

Though this story is outlandish, the point of it is: no two days are the same. This is one of the reasons why I chose the profession. Most days have a more positive outcome than having their facilities trashed and guns pointed at them, but I wouldn't trade this job for any other job in the world.

In fact, I couldn't imagine doing anything else.

CHAPTER 2

The Aftermath of a Suicide

Ken's Story

I f you open your own place, you'll fail, and commit suicide just like your father."

Those are the exact words Dick said to me when I told him my plans of quitting his employ and going out on my own and opening a mortuary.

Nice guy, huh?

The memory of those words still makes my blood boil, but I think they are why I have succeeded. It was a personal challenge; I took those words and embraced them in a death grip—like a python squeezing its prey.

It's no secret that my interest in this profession formed because of a tragedy that befell me at a young age. My dad committed suicide when I was twelve. The compassion of the funeral director that handled my dad's services sealed my fate. I don't think that's a unique phenomenon at all; I have come across scores of other funeral directors throughout the years who say they were called into the profession after experiencing a death in the family and seeing the ministry the funeral director provided.

The most vivid memory I have surrounding my dad's death is

Charlotte's Web. My parents were separated and my brother, Kevin, and I were at my dad's apartment the night before his death, watching TV, and *Charlotte's Web* was on. Of course my dad was on the phone, fighting with my mom, while we were parked on the moss-green Berber carpet watching the color tube in the wood cabinet. It was a serial, so after a half hour, heavy with commercial breaks, the announcer said something to the effect of, "Tune in tomorrow for the exciting conclusion..." When the show ended my parents were still fighting.

The next day, Dad, a physical therapist, dropped Kevin and me off at Pioneer Park Pool on his way to work. We stood in the dusty parking lot watching him drive off, a comical scene because he was six-seven and usually drove around in an MG Midget. It was during the gas crisis and the Midget was easy on gas, but he still looked like he was riding around in a clown car. That was the last time I ever saw him, his hulking frame wedged into that tiny blue MG, its taillights receding down the boulevard. I didn't linger on the sight—Kevin and I were too eager to get inside where my other siblings were already waiting for us.

Mom was supposed to pick us up, and when she didn't come, the four of us, standing in our dripping swimsuits in the gravel parking lot, shrugged and raced back inside the gates. We were thrilled Mom was late; it was a rare treat to get to stay late at the pool. Finally, a family friend, Karen, came to pick us up.

We were splashing around when Karen came in and systematically rounded us up one by one. I remember that for some strange reason, Karen's daughter was crying, but I was too young to sense the tension in the car, and happily rode to the farm where we lived, making fun of Renée for crying.

I grew up on a farm in Nevada City, a small city located between Reno and Sacramento on Route 80, at the base of the Sierra Nevada mountains. The farm wasn't a commercial farm, but it was a working farm. We raised livestock and crops for personal consumption. That's where Dad did it, at the farm. As Karen drove down the gravel drive, I saw a bunch of strange vehicles parked in the yard and my mom standing in the porch. She had the most peculiar look on her face.

And all of the sudden I knew why Renée was crying.

Someone was dead.

"Kids, I have something to tell you..." my mom said, in the yard on bended knee. The four of us clustered around her.

After the initial emotional and physical frenzy, I asked her, "What happened? How did Dad die?"

"Wouldn't you rather just remember him as you knew him?" she asked, deflecting.

"No," I said stubbornly. "I want to know."

She looked at me for a long minute, her face red and streaked with tears, and finally said, "He shot himself, Kenny."

All at once I felt myself in that "vacuum" of space the recently bereaved seem to enter into, where I was emotionless, and puzzled by that fact. I knew I should be upset, but I felt like I was a million miles from anything, save the words: *He shot himself, Kenny.*

I was totally weightless, floating in outer space, with those words repeating in the periphery. *He shot himself, Kenny.*

Later that night, I found myself back in my Dad's apartment, parked on the green carpeting, watching the conclusion to *Charlotte's Web* for a lack of anything better to do. I remember thinking to myself, *I started this show with Dad alive, and now as it ends...*

Nevada City was such a small place that my dad had dated the funeral director, Paula Bateman, in high school. After high school Paula had married the man that ran the local funeral home and when he died she took it over and ran it on a widow's license.

Paula, bless her soul, put up with the curiosities and incessant questions of a twelve-year-old during what must have been, for her too, a very hard time. It can be a very emotional time for me, these days, when I handle services for a friend who has died of natural causes. I can't imagine what Paula was going through emotionally as she handled the funeral arrangements for a man whom she probably loved for a short time, who had met with a sudden and violent end.

I have this vivid memory of my dad lying in his casket. He looked like himself, but because he was such a vigorous man in life, it was odd to see him so still. People say things to the effect of "She doesn't look like herself" and I don't think they can necessarily put their finger on *why* that person lying in repose doesn't look like the person they knew. In most cases it's not the physical appearance, it's the stillness, the complete and total lack of animation. I know that's what it was for my dad—the stillness.

Though it was a little unnerving and upsetting seeing my dad, I'll forever thank my mom for letting me view him. A lot of parents would want to shelter their children from that, especially thirty years ago, but my mom was progressive in that respect. The upset feeling faded quickly as I worked through my grief (some days I feel like I'm still working through it on some level), but I still retain that picture in my mind of him, laid out in his suit, looking so peaceful.

The catharsis of it all came at the repast, held at the farmhouse. The cleaning crew had worked hard to clean the scene up and there were still giant, industrial fans blowing in the house to try to dry out the carpeting, among other things. Bored with all the adults and their plates of salads and cold cuts and hushed talk, Kevin had the bright idea of seeing what would happen if he tossed a piece of toilet paper behind the fan. The giant metal blades shredded it and sent out millions of little pieces like snow.

Well, that was it. We began grabbing huge handfuls of toilet paper and tossing them behind the fans and watching in delight as they chewed them up and spit out toilet paper snow upon all the black-clad mourners. I hadn't laughed so hard before then, nor do I think I will ever laugh so hard again. The mourners sat there, plates balanced precariously on their knees, taking our punishment because nobody wanted to be the one to yell at the kids who had just lost their father.

Because I grew up on a farm, I was no stranger to driving tractors and other pieces of machinery from a young age. It wasn't unusual for my mom to say, "Kenny, can you back your dad's truck up to the barn and clean it out and wash it? Mr. McGee will be by later in the day to pick it up." The GMC Jimmy had sat idle for the three weeks after my dad's death, until my mom decided she didn't want to look at it anymore and ran an ad in *The Union*, the local newspaper, and sold the truck.

I dutifully trotted out to the truck and climbed in. When I reached down to rack the seat forward my hand brushed something strange and square. I pulled out the cube of Styrofoam holding forty-nine .45 ACP rounds. One hole, the one in the corner, was missing a bullet. Instinctively, I knew what I was holding. I felt like I was choking. Carefully, I laid the cube on the passenger seat, and sat in the interior warmed by summer sun, studying the dust motes. After a few minutes the overwhelming choking sensation passed, and I cranked the engine. The engine turned over a few times before catching, and when it did, the eight-track player clicked on, and Cher's cover of Bob Dylan's "All I Really Want to Do" blasted through the speakers. That was the last song Dad had listened to. When that thought popped into my head, the choking sensation returned, and it was a few moments before I was able to collect myself and engage the clutch. Those sensations of choking eventually became less frequent and

severe, then disappeared altogether, and I know now that physical manifestations like that are a normal part of the grieving
process.

Somehow the whole experience surrounding Dad's death and
watching how Paula handled everything rattled around in my
brain for the next few years. By the time I graduated from high
school all those ideas had congealed into what I knew my purpose in life was: I was going to be a funeral director.

I registered as an apprentice with the State of California when
I was twenty. My first job was with Lakewood Memorial Park in
Modesto. I was the typical apprentice; I did all the grunt work
like sweeping the parking lot, emptying ashtrays, and running errands. But I also started learning how to embalm, and to conduct services. Looking back, I did an inordinate amount of
graveside services, and I think it's because Modesto is in the
middle of the state and it gets hot there. Nobody else wanted to
stand in 110-degree heat, so why not send the apprentice? And
let me tell you, those cemetery tents trap the heat and make it ten
times worse! The sweat would just roll down my back during all
those gravesides.

The one thing they wouldn't let me do, however, was make funeral arrangements. The manager said I looked too young. At
twenty, I probably looked fifteen. This is something I would hear
many times during my career until I opened up my own place—
you look too young! This is the only profession that seems to be
an "old man's game." There are a lot of jobs out there that you
hear are a "young man's game" because you need the strength
and stamina and whatnot to do the job, but undertaking is the
opposite. When I would be out with a part-timer, who are generally retired from their careers and work just to stay busy in
their golden years, the family members would always turn to the
part-timer and ask questions, only to have the part-timer defer to

me. This is something that I still see to this day; the public seems to gravitate toward the more "mature" members of the staff. It's just a stereotype that undertakers are all old crusty, fussy fossils.

I didn't stay at Lakewood Memorial long. I moved to Fry Memorial Chapel in Manteca, where I worked for a few months. It was a little different. Fry was just a mortuary; it didn't have the cemetery like Lakewood did. I decided the middle of the state was too hot and made the move to Los Angeles after only about a year at Fry.

It was a real culture shock going from a sleepy little town to a major American city. I attended Cypress Mortuary College and worked for a mortuary I'll call "Lotus Chapel" that was owned by a larger corporation.

It was a decent gig. In exchange for free room, I was on call about three nights a week. The house was a separate building from the mortuary, so it was like I had my own place. And in the true fashion of a freewheeling young man, I hardly saved a dime those eight years I was with Lotus Chapel. Overall, that was a great period of my life. I was making a decent living, had few responsibilities outside of work, and my whole paycheck was gravy. Why would I ever want the headache of small business ownership?

Then the AIDS epidemic hit.

I don't really think of myself as an *activist*. I'm not nearly that radical, but I slowly became disenchanted with what I was seeing as injustices going on in my community. It was the early nineties, which was a scary time in some respects. AIDS was peaking, and even though there was much more information than there had been ten, even five years prior, there was still a lot of misinformation floating around. California has a large homosexual population and there were a large number of gay people dying from the virus. Lotus Chapel was charging a biohazard fee to people suspected of having AIDS—namely homosexuals—but not to anyone else. At this point, the profession had implemented a workplace health initiative called "universal precautions" to protect the funeral practitioner from potential diseases from *any* human remains. Basically, the mantra of universal precautions is: treat every body like has an infectious disease.

Theoretically, every case should have been treated the same, but certain families were getting hit with a biohazard fee, and others weren't. I didn't think that was fair. Subconsciously this could've really gotten under my skin because I'm a gay man, but I'd like to think the real reason is because I got into this profession to help people. And seeing people in one of their greatest times of need being treated unfairly just plain rubbed me the wrong way.

That's when I decided to open my own place, and that's when "Richard," whom I'll call "Dick" for short, made his famous statement to me.

I wish I could say I told Dick to fuck off and then went out and proved him wrong by setting the world on fire. That wouldn't be the case.

When I quit Lotus Chapel, I had identified a space in an industrial tilt-style building on Orange Avenue in the Signal Hill area. The contractor I hired to outfit the mixed commercial space was, in typical contractor fashion, behind schedule. The day I quit I went to my new office to find nothing but studs. The space was supposed to have been finished at this point, but didn't even have drywall! In the State of California you can't get a facility permit to conduct the business of funeral directing until your building has been inspected as a proper facility.

For the next ninety days I sat around just thinking, *What the hell did you do?* while the contractor moved at the comparative speed of an email versus a pony express rider delivering mail cross-country: SLOW.

Finally, McKenzie Services opened in 1994. Signal Hill is an old town in California and doesn't permit funeral homes or mortuaries within the municipality. Working with some very shrewd people at town hall, "McKenzie Cremation and Burial Services" was able to secure a business license because technically we were neither a dreaded funeral home nor mortuary, and in order to keep any feathers from getting ruffled, I decided it would be prudent to have the business sign say just "McKenzie Services."

So there I was in this mixed commercial building made out of poured concrete, an espresso machine manufacturer next door, and Head Start headquarters next to that. I certainly didn't look like any of my contemporaries with their beautiful mansions sitting on perfectly manicured grounds surrounded by a gleaming fleet of hearses and SUVs. I was just a storefront with two arrangements offices, a business office, embalming room, and tiny viewing room where people could view their loved one prior to cremation.

In those early years I liken myself to a nineteenth-century undertaker, in that I did most of my work outside of what I affectionately called the "shop." All the visitations and services were held in area churches, chapels, and halls. I like to think that during those years I introduced families to churches and churches to families. There are over 120 churches in the greater Signal Hill area, and until I moved the business to its current location in 2005, I rotated services and viewings around to all the churches.

It's a fact of life that in my business, one has to break in with "discount work," essentially undercutting the established firms to cull their business. I offered sharply reduced prices compared to my competitors, but never thought of my business as a discount firm. I offered good service at a great value, and still do (so says I). Perhaps the greatest affirmation of setting out on my own was when an AIDS family would come in and ask me what my biohazard fee was. I'd reply, "I don't have one." The establishment had so conditioned these families that they were different they were flabbergasted when I affirmed what they knew all along—they should be treated the same as everyone else.

Back in the nineties I probably handled twenty AIDS cases a month. Due to better antiretrovirals and combination therapies, people living with this terrible disease can live much longer and more fulfilling lives, and I hardly handle any AIDS cases anymore. The irony isn't lost on me that I built my business on the Golden Rule: treat people as you'd like to be treated.

As I mentioned earlier, the original incarnation of the business was called McKenzie Cremation and Burial Services, but when I moved to Long Beach in 2005 I changed the name to McKenzie Mortuary, the name I'd always wanted to call the business but couldn't due to the laws of Signal Hill. McKenzie Mortuary: it's a simple enough name that combines my surname with the type of business. I don't know if I subconsciously picked this name because of childhood stories that leached into the bedrock of my psyche, but my *dad*—yes, the dad who died seventeen years before I opened the business—came up with the name.

Todd has a little more family history in the business than I, but *every* family, it seems, has some sort of connection with our business. Mine included. My great-grandmother used to work as a hostess at a funeral parlor in Nevada City. A hostess is someone who works the visitations, usually standing in the lobby greeting visitors, asking people to sign the guest book, and taking coats. My great-grandmother had a real wry sense of humor and used to refer to herself (in the privacy of our family—certainly not to the public) as a "stiff sitter." My dad, who I think got his sense of humor from her, would answer the phone at the farm, "McKenzie Mortuary, you stab 'em, we slab 'em!" Though I don't think the name of my business carries the glibness of my dad's phone salutation, I believe in some small way he did name my business. Or at least, I like thinking that.

Ironically, the funeral parlor my great-grandmother worked at was the same funeral parlor where my dad was laid out, though long before Mr. Bateman or his wife, Paula, ran it.

I think my first big break came a little less than a year after I opened McKenzie Services. I was hosting my first ever estate sale and the *Press Telegram* sent a reporter, Robyn Hynch, to cover the story—must've been a slow news day. I got talking to Robyn and she ended up doing a human-interest feature piece on my new business.

A sign above him explains that proceeds will go to AIDS hospices. This isn't your ordinary sale, but then McKenzie's not your ordinary mortician. He's become expert at taking the business of death and finding a positive somewhere in its midst...If he keeps it up, he may single-handedly restore public trust in a business badly damaged by [redacted] fiasco. Maybe he'll get a well-deserved pat on the back from the peers who told him he'd never make it.

In chemistry they call this the activation energy, or the energy needed to get the reaction going. Her piece was the push that got my business going, and I'll always be grateful to her for doing that for me.

I quickly outgrew my small shop in Signal Hill and purchased a plot of land on Anaheim Street in Long Beach in 2003. The plot contained a restaurant and two houses, which I tore down to build my existing mortuary from the ground up. I have occupied the building since 2005, and while running my tiny burgeoning business out of a storefront was something of an adventure for my younger self, it is heaven having a dedicated mortuary building, complete with chapel, that I custom designed to my liking.

I wouldn't say I've arrived. In this business, you never arrive, you just depart—I know, corny joke, but the closest I've come was in 2007. The California Funeral Director's Association voted me "Outstanding Funeral Director" of the year. And even though I have a saying about awards and hemorrhoids, it was a pretty big honor for me. There are a lot of funeral directors in my state.

At the awards ceremony in Oakland, when my name was called and I got onstage, I knew I had arrived when I spied Dick in the front row, standing and applauding.

That was the moment I got my pat on the back. That was the moment I decided I could let it go.

CHAPTER 3

The Label: Undertaker

Todd's Story

I like the label undertaker.

It's more visceral than the alternative.

People tend to shy away from it because it connotes the body "going under"—like a burial—when in fact the name originated because the undertaker *undertook* the tasks necessary to properly bury a person. In 1882 the National Funeral Directors Association* got together for their first annual meeting and decided to officially change the professional title from undertaker to funeral director. Somehow, that vestige has stuck. Undertaker is still common terminology to the public, and within the profession itself. Maybe it has stuck because people prefer the darker tone the name suggests and how it fits with the

---

*The genesis of the NFDA, or National Funeral Directors Association, can be traced to a group of Michigan undertakers in 1880 who formed the Association of Funeral Directors, the first such state association for the profession. In 1881 they changed their name to the Michigan Funeral Directors Association. A year later they met with other newly formed state associations and formed the NFDA, an organization still in existence today.

tasks, the undertakings, we complete. But with the way our country loves to be politically correct, and the American attitude toward death, I wouldn't be surprised if, when I retire, I won't have some new label like *Memorial Event Planner, Last Rites Coordinator,* or even something fun sounding like *Final Celebration Arranger.* But that's fine, no matter what label they slap on it, it's still the same profession. We prepare the dead for their final journey and help their families honor them in a fitting way. Because, at that point, that's all the dead have left: the memories of them.

I got into this business the way most people do: family. I wasn't born into it though, like most of the people who go into the business. My mom is a teacher and my dad is a pilot (who has an uncomfortable relationship with the dead). Uncle Rick is the family undertaker.

I went off to college and, like most of my generation, wasn't quite sure where my place in the world was going to be. First, I thought I'd like to be a doctor, and then a research scientist, and then maybe a CSI, and then a pharmacist—essentially I didn't know, but something in the sciences. One by one I checked them off the list. Each one was missing something that I think, in retrospect, I have identified as the "human element." Yes, those professionals all interact with people as a matter of their daily routine, but it's secondary to the job.

So I was drifting after college and needed a little cash and asked my uncle if I could do some odd jobs at the funeral home. He gave me a couple of jobs, and I enjoyed hanging around the funeral home. And now readers may be thinking to themselves *how can someone enjoy hanging around a funeral home?* Partly, it goes back to the point of the story about Ken's riot: no day is the same. The truth is the job chose me, not the other way around. The work fit. Much like you hear a minister answering "a calling," it was kind of like that—but not as dramatic. It was an organic fit. Uncle Rick hired me on full-time and I've never looked back.

I had the pleasure of learning the profession at the right hand of someone I believe to be, hands down, one of the best practitioners in the field: Uncle Rick. He eats, sleeps, and breathes what he does, which is more than I can say. Though I enjoy what I do, what he does defines him. Uncle Rick is one of those lucky people who grew up knowing exactly what he wanted to do. Ever since he was a little kid he had one goal in mind: be a funeral director. Uncle Rick used to host funerals with neighborhood kids using shoeboxes as caskets and dead birds he'd found as the guests of honor. He even insisted on a black bike so it could be like the black hearses he saw.

Even when I encounter his old classmates from elementary school (at funerals, where else?) they still say, "I remember him telling me he wanted to be an undertaker even in [insert a number] grade. Can you imagine?"

What's wrong with a boy who has his career path picked out?

Nothing. It's the idea that someone would *want* to work with the dead. Maybe it's perspective. I can't imagine anyone wanting to do tax returns, collect garbage, perform colonoscopies, or embark on an illustrious telemarketing career. I find fulfillment from what I do, much like an accountant might find satisfaction from the financial health and balanced ledger of a client, and like the accountant, at the end of the day, I turn the lights off, lock the door, and go home to my family. I think what I'm trying to say is that we all have our own callings. And though they may seem a little different to each other, they play to our strengths—I sure as hell couldn't talk someone into buying a WaterPik over the phone. My aptitude, though, may be genetic. I come from a lineage of undertakers.

There are only two photographs remaining of my great-great grandfather, Isaac White. One, taken near the end of his life, depicts him and his wife, Rachel, standing on the front porch of their home, which also served as the town's only funeral parlor and was aptly named Isaac White, Undertaker and Funeral Director. Isaac's boots are dusty, probably after a long day spent in some rural cemetery where he more than likely helped the men of the bereaved family fill the grave, shovelful by shovelful, before retiring back to the churchyard—first taking his horse team (black for adults, white for children) back to the livery—for the repast.

Typical of photographs of the time, neither Rachel nor Isaac is smiling. People lived harder lives then. Isaac's beard is long and white, hanging all the way down to the pocket watch chain in his vest. But the beard isn't just the typical fashion statement of the mid-nineteenth century; it covered the smallpox scars on his face, and the all-black undertaker's suit covered the other scars from the battlefield.

Isaac was an infantry soldier in the Union Army, and saw innumerable horrific things unfold as his countrymen slaughtered each other. He saw death up close, and in a gruesome fashion few people have to experience. And, ironically, it was the bloody Civil War that set the stage for Isaac's profession. American embalming pioneers like Thomas Holmes and Richard Burr embalmed the remains of wealthy soldiers on the battlefields so they could be returned to their families for a proper burial. But the assassination of President Lincoln, his subsequent embalming, and the twenty days before his burial is what tipped embalming into public favor. The public had previously regarded embalming—or scientific preservation—with suspicion before Lincoln's funeral train, but after witnessing how lifelike he looked even after almost three weeks postmortem,* Americans embraced the "new science."†

Isaac returned to the sleepy town of Milford, Delaware, after the war, where he eventually joined his brother Harrison in business, having taken the company over from their father, James, a tradesman undertaker and local cabinetmaker. In the 1870 census—before he joined his brother—Isaac's profession is listed as "carpenter." This skill would serve him well in later years, for men in the trade in his generation had to make their own caskets and coffins (the difference: four versus six sides). It would be some years before specialized casket (and shroud) companies would start mass-producing their wares, and could feasibly transport commercial caskets. Running a funeral parlor was very much a family vocation in the nineteenth century, and still remains so to a degree today. As such, Rachel, Isaac's wife, sewed the casket interiors. There are still a number of mom-and-pop shops today where the husband (traditionally) does the funeral directing and the wife does everything from housekeeping to bookkeeping.

Though it is still very much a family business, things have changed a lot since Isaac's time; he died of Bright's Disease only sixteen years after automobiles became commercially available. And despite the fact that technology has changed the way we conduct business, the fundamental nature of our profession remains the same: we prepare the dead for their journey to their

---

*Undertakers at each stop would "touch up" the president.
†Europeans had been experimenting with various forms of embalming for several hundred years before the American Civil War.

final earthly destination and offer comfort to those they leave behind. You don't need a big fancy hearse to do that. Isaac used a wagon.

So why mention my great-great-grandfather, an undertaker who has been dead for nearly a century? The business is one that tends to be passed down generation to generation. But even if not, almost everyone has a member of this age-old profession in his or her lineage, one just has to look back far enough. There is evidence of early man performing funeral rites, but the designation of an actual person (or in the case of the Egyptians, a cadre of people) whose sole job was to handle the dead didn't come about until about four thousand years ago with the Egyptians. Which begs another question, why is the profession tagged with this stigma? What stigma, you ask? The stigma of *wanting* to work around the dead.

Is there something unnatural about caring for our dead? The Egyptian embalmers were revered and shunned at the same time. Sadly, things haven't changed much since then. If my wife is asked what her husband does she generally gets a response to the effect of, "He does what?" [Insert puzzled look] "And you're okay with that?"

What's she supposed to say? It's what I do, and it's the only thing she's ever known me to do. I can think of a lot stranger, and more unnatural, things to do off the top of my head, or you can just flip on the TV and watch an episode of *Dirty Jobs*.

What's unnatural about caring for our dead?

To use a common catchphrase, "we're a necessary evil." Necessary because death is a 100 percent certainty, and evil because the undertaker's mere presence is a reminder of your own mortality. The fact is, it's never a joyous occasion when our services are needed. Joyous or not, *everyone* needs funeral rites.

I think Jessica Mitford can best sum up the American attitude toward the profession: "I have nothing against undertakers personally, I just wouldn't want one to take care of my sister."

My response is, "Then who will?"

And, suddenly, the stigmatized profession begins to make a little more sense. We'll just have to see what the next four thousand years brings. Maybe by then your computer will be able to do the job.

Technology has made an unexpected impact on this profession in recent years—not from the practitioner's standpoint but from the public's. It has made grieving more convenient. Drive-through viewings, electronic guest books, webcasted funerals, e-condolences, and 1-800-Flowers, hell, you don't even have to step foot into a funeral home anymore if you don't want to. Death is being made nice and convenient and sanitary, if you want. We no longer have figurative cemetery dust on our boots. In fact, a lot of times, the family doesn't even watch the casket being lowered.

What will this convenience mean for us in the long run? I don't know, because I worry that ease can aid denial. If you can point and click and be done with it, did you really acknowledge that death? Some may argue so, but I argue that convenience *doesn't* equate to ease when talking about grief. Simply put: you can't make a journey without taking any steps.

Acknowledging the death is the first step in the healing process, so if we continue to sit behind our computer screens and scroll through our smart phones, being too busy to grieve properly, we may just become a nation of perpetually grieving people.

Or not.

But hey, I hear technology is doing great things. Maybe it'll eliminate grief and death and the undertaker altogether. But I doubt it.

After our first book, *Mortuary Confidential: Undertakers Spill the Dirt,* came out it was amazing how many people approached me to share their stories. Whether it was how they had swept the sidewalk at the local funeral home as a kid, washed the cars, or something out of the ordinary that happened at a funeral they attended, or just their experience with a death, everyone has something to share about the subject. That's the thing about death: we all dread it rearing its ugly head in our lives, but it is something *everybody* experiences. As humans, I think it's something that connects us, unexpectedly at times. We don't all get married, or travel, or go to school, or have children, or have a host of other experiences, but no matter what country you are from or your economic status, you are connected to this piece of the human condition: death.

And while we, the practitioners, purvey death on a daily basis, it certainly doesn't steel us to the emotional blow that is the passing of a loved one. Ken's mother and grandmother died during the writing of the first book, and during one of our many conversations he said to me, "I've been doing this for over twenty years, and there was nothing, *nothing,* I could've done to prepare myself for seeing my mother dead."

It can be very conflicting, knowing intellectually how the bereaved feel, and then when a loved one dies experiencing that loss primally. The funeral director generally doesn't have an emotional connection for the same reason a surgeon can't operate on a family member. The emotions can get in the way of best interests of the bereaved. We certainly sympathize, but can't empathize, unless the loss belongs to us, and then we move from the role of funeral director to the role of bereaved.

But even though we can't join the families in the trenches of grief we all give up little pieces of ourselves.

I live and work in a moderately populated city, but one that still retains the small-community feel. Frigyes Karinthy, the Hungarian author, put forth the theory that anyone is separated from anyone else in the world by only six degrees of separation. There's a colloquialism where I live in Wilmington that there's only a single degree of separation. It's a pretty small place. So, rare is it a funeral that I don't see a single soul I know walking through the door. But that's good. I can't imagine practicing somewhere so big and impersonal as New York City, because in addition to caring for the dead, you'll generally find your local funeral director to be something of a civic leader. And, being such, it's nice to know the people of your community when they walk through the door.

The friends and acquaintances that come to a funeral invariably ask later, "What exactly is it you do? I saw you just standing around looking pretty."

Yes, everyone sees the expensive suits and fancy cars and stoic demeanors. But really, what do I do? I could tell you some technical bullshit or about the bureaucratic largesse of rules, regs, and paperwork, but that's not it. I think the true essence of this profession can be summed up with a little anecdote.

I like to work with my hands. I'm certainly no Bob Vila, but I know my way around a hammer and nail. Among other things, I probably inherited a little of Isaac's carpentry blood. My wife says it's an emotional release of sorts: after absorbing the problems of the dead and bereaved all day I come home and spend some time working in solitude. We had bought a house that hadn't had any updating to it since Lyndon Johnson's administration, so I was like a kid in a candy shop: I didn't know what to do next.

It was autumn and I had gutted a bathroom and figured I could turn it around in three or four days, right? Wrong. It's just the nature of the beast, and the beast reared its head. I really can't remember us ever being this busy. And in between working nighttime viewings, days off, my regular weekends, and weekends I was supposed to be off, my gutted bathroom sat and sat. I'm kind of neurotic when it comes to projects. Once I've started, I work and work until it's finished. I'm not one of those people that can just let things languish. I like to get things back in order.

This bathroom was driving me crazy.

I wasn't complaining—because I know it's the job—but I was bemoaning to coworkers, saying things like, "I was going to lay the floor last night. All I needed was a couple hours, but I got held up because of—"

I remember it distinctly. It was a young person's funeral. One of those sad situations where there were young children left as survivors. The funeral was packed, and to say it was a sad occasion would be an understatement. During the service, a colleague and I were standing in the narthex (that's fancy funeral-director speak for a church's lobby) watching the proceedings. He leaned over to me and said, "Your bathroom doesn't seem so important now, does it?"

He was right.

And that is what we do. We are whom you call to guide you through that crisis. We are the face of the ritual and pomp that surrounds the last great ceremony of someone's time here on earth, and we forsake our personal lives to do it . . . because we care, no, *believe in,* what we do enough to relinquish pieces of ourselves to those we serve. Because it is important. The dead, believe it or not, play a vital role in our society. If the dead didn't matter, that would mean you wouldn't matter, and that just isn't true. We, the undertakers, make sure of that.

Yes, we believe in what we do, but at the end of the day belief alone isn't going to put bread on the table. It is a business. It's not always easy to transact business when there's been a death, and people cry foul. "Undertakers take advantage of people when they are at their most vulnerable!" I know people who have been called "thief," "vulture," and "bloodsucker" to their faces. To those throwing the insults, I ask, "When was the last time you worked for free?" We just ask remuneration for services provided, nothing else. There are laws in place to protect the consumer, not just for this profession but also from the myriad of other unsavory men and women in other businesses out there.

But for those who wish to hurl names at us bloodsuckers, I have a piece of folklore about Isaac. I'm not going to toot my horn; it doesn't seem to hold as much gravity.

A man walked from his farm to the familiar (ironically) white-colored house in the center of town leading a milk cow. He tied the length of rope that was around the beast's neck to the sign advertising UNDERTAKING and FUNERAL DIRECTING and knocked on the front door. Rachel received him and offered him something cool to drink while she went to fetch Isaac in his woodshop. The man obliged. When Isaac finally came out onto the porch, wiping the wood dust from his hands on his pants, the man said, "I've brought this milk cow as payment for my wife's burial."

Isaac took him by the arm and led him down the steps and said, "You've got a newborn that needs to eat. You take this beast back home, and if you can ever pay me then pay me. In the meantime, your daughter needs this cow's milk more than I do."

The man persisted.

Isaac insisted.

The man relented and took his milk cow home to feed the motherless infant.

The point of that little piece of lore is simply that this profession isn't a job, it's a calling, and when death does occur there is someone to call who isn't doing it for the money, but because he or she believes everyone is entitled to a proper, dignified burial.

And someone needs to undertake that job.

CHAPTER 4

Foray into Fund-Raising

I guess you could say it all started with Paul dying at the Veteran's Hospital in Long Beach. His children flew in from Denmark to help their mother make the funeral arrangements. We had the funeral a few days later—on a fine, sunny California day—and his children flew back. Three days after their departure, Paul's wife, Ellen died. His children, having just arrived home in Denmark, made the trek back across the puddle and the continent to Signal Hill, California, to have another funeral. On their first visit they had stayed for several weeks to help their mother with things and visit with her. In the European culture they seem to be a bit more laid-back as far as vacation time goes than here in America, but the children had professional and familial obligations back in their country and couldn't dally for a second time in a row.

"I don't know what I'm going to do," Peter, Paul and Ellen's son, lamented to me at the restaurant after the funeral. The family had invited me out to eat with them. "It's going to be months before I'll be able to get back here and start going through Mom and Dad's things."

I could imagine. It's not like Denmark is around the corner from Long Beach. "What are you going to do?" I asked, making conversation more than anything else.

"Give everything away," he said. "Anne and I have homes. We don't need anything, and even if we did it would be more practical to buy it there than ship anything halfway across the world."

"And there's nothing of real value in the house," Anne said in her perfect English. She had been born in America, but had enough European tendencies that her flawless English surprised me every time she opened her mouth. "Peter is right. We just need to give everything away."

An idea popped into my head. "Tell you what," I said. "I'll clean their house out for you—for free—with the stipulation that anything I sell I get to donate the proceeds to a charity of my choice. Obviously," I added hastily, "any family photos or personal mementos I'll set aside, and the next time you are in the States"—I parroted a term I'd heard them use—"I'll give it to you. Then you can just put the empty house on the market."

"Brilliant!" Anne said, clapping her hands.

"What a relief," Peter said, looking almost too relieved.

This is great, I thought. *It'll be a cinch. I'll box up some photos, sell their furniture, and raise some money for AIDS Walk Long Beach.*

I was wrong.

I quickly discovered why Peter was so relieved that I was taking this task off his hands. He was already four thousand miles away by the time I got around to going over to Paul and Ellen's house. It was just a modest rancher, not overly large by most standards, but when I pushed the front door open the words out of my mouth were "Oh my God!" The place was a hoarder's lair. There was stuff everywhere, with little pathways winding through the house like the trench system of the first Great War.

It took me months, but in the end the house was empty. Over the three plus months I worked on emptying the house, I enlisted the help of friends and family, calling in all the favors I had ever banked in my life. By the end, I had a nice pile of items for a tag sale, a small pile for Peter and Anne, and I had given the garbage men quite the workout. Every Monday and Thursday there was a mountain of old newspapers and magazines, broken electronics, clothes that would never be considered retro, furniture beyond repair, and *junk*.

"Estate Sale: Benefiting AIDS Walk Long Beach," the fliers bragged that I plastered the neighborhood around my business with. The day of the sale I rented a truck to haul all the stuff over to McKenzie Services. I figured I'd attract a lot more business in a more commercial area than the suburbs where Paul and Ellen's house was. The contents of their home stretched the entire length of the sidewalk; it was a bargain seeker's delight. As I mentioned previously, Robyn Hynch from the *Press Telegram* showed up to do an article about it.

The first estate sale, done solely with items from Paul and Ellen's house, was so successful—it raised $2,900, a formidable sum in 1995—I decided to continue the tradition each year. "By mid-afternoon Sunday, he counted $1,800 in his cash box, not including what he'll make in the yet-to-be-sold antique clothing, stamp, and toy collections. You can bet this won't be that last AIDS sales he'll organize," Robyn wrote in her article. It certainly wasn't the last one; Robyn had helped me create a "monster."

Ancient Chinese philosopher and general Sun Tzu said in *The Art of War,* "Opportunities multiply when they are seized." Boy, did the opportunities continue to multiply . . . and exponentially multiply, *sine die.*

After the wildly successful first estate sale, families would say, "Mom (or Dad) has a lot of furniture and we're not going to want it all so we're donating the rest to your sale." I don't want to sound ungrateful. I'm not, in fact, I'm the opposite, grateful and humbled by people's generosity, but don't forget I was running a mortuary out of a tiny storefront. I had no place to put all the donations! But what could I say? I couldn't turn down such generosity, especially when the solicitations were never phrased as questions.

We jammed stuff into every free square inch of McKenzie Services, filled my garage, basement, attic, and all my friends' and families' homes I could impose upon, until it got so ridiculous that I began renting storage units to put all the stuff. That's when the wheels came off the operation. The rental units were expensive and began to really eat into the bottom line of the money raised from the sale. We took a several-year hiatus from the estate sales until we moved into the much larger facility in Long Beach. After many successful years, the estate sale simply became a victim of its own success.

About the time I was (no pun intended) tabling the estate sale because of lack of room, something annoying was buzzing in my ear like that gnat that homes in on you when you're at a backyard party on a hot summer afternoon and won't leave you alone no matter what corner of the yard you run to, or how hard you corkscrew your ear. The buzz wouldn't go away. It just kept getting louder and louder. The buzz was a little show called *Six Feet Under*, and *everybody* was talking about it.

"Have you seen this new show on HBO—?"

"Have you heard about this undertaker show—?"

"There's this show...and someone dies a different way at the beginning of each—"

I don't watch too much TV; I seem to spend a lot of time at the mortuary, but finally I caved and watched this show *everybody* was talking about. ("Oh, Ken you simply *must* watch *Six Feet Under*. You'll love it!") It's about a family of funeral directors in, of all places, Los Angeles. And, one of the funeral directors is gay.

I remember lying on my couch, half-stoned from a Downeaster—vodka, cranberry, and pineapple—but thinking to myself, *this show is great!* Then and there a great fund-raiser for AIDS Walk Long Beach popped into my head. It was a big, bold idea, but I'm impulsive, so I acted on it.

I held the *Six Feet Under* premier party for the second season premier on March 3, 2002. The party was set up to look like a typical funeral service meets Hollywood party, in a church of course, because I was still in my small shop in Signal Hill.

Just like a Hollywood premier, a giant searchlight, pointed skyward, advertised the event to the neighborhood. In front of the Little Brown Chapel I had parked my hearse, surrounded it with red velvet ropes, and hired a professional photographer to photograph people coming in on the red carpet. When the guests entered the narthex, they saw that in the place we might hold a viewing there were caskets, but not the way one might expect. I had a buffet built around the open caskets so it looked like the table was almost part of them. It was deliciously *Addams Family* kitschy. In the sanctuary, instead of the traditional single casket at the front of the church there were six closed caskets, containing yet-to-be-unveiled prizes. The guests mingled and nibbled at the casket buffet until showtime.

The church has one of those large screens that comes down

from the ceiling, so the audience watched the season premier of *Six Feet Under* like they were seated for a funeral service. The sanctuary was packed. At the conclusion of the show, I played the part of Monty Hall, the host of *Let's Make a Deal,* and contestants came up with the chance to win what was in the six caskets up front: prizes, cash, or nothing. It was a huge success. The total turnout was over five hundred people, including special guest star and actor Tim Maculan, who plays Father Jack in the series. I raised $7,000 for AIDS Walk Long Beach that night.

GET READY TO GO SIX FEET UNDER. FOR CHARITY, THAT IS was the headline in the *Press Telegram.*

MORTUARY RAISES MONEY WITH HBO TV SERIES was the headline of *The Signal.*

Still fresh off the smashing success of that fund-raiser, I flew too close to the sun, and made the worst financial decision of my life. I decided to do a benefit calendar.

The idea to make a calendar wasn't as impulsive as my decision to do the *Six Feet Under* party, but it was close. It all began sometime in 2004 when my long-time best friend, Keegan Mac-Cahill, began battling cancer. I drove up to San Francisco to spend some time with her. While there she began to tell me about this idea she had to employ women undergoing cancer therapy. She wanted to create a clothing company called Chemosabe* and make bandannas at first and maybe branch out into other clothes. The clothing wasn't the important thing, per se—the important thing was employing other women undergoing the same struggles as she was. It's hard to work when

---

*A little research revealed there already was a company out there named Chemosabe making head coverings.

you're going through chemotherapy. Not only do you not feel well enough to work most of the time, the treatments are time-consuming. A lot of people have to stop working, and the medical bills start piling up. Keegan is like me in the way that she has these wild ideas. I thought it was a great idea.

Sometime during my visit we were shopping at the Westfield Centre and Keegan stopped at one of those ubiquitous calendar kiosks you find in all malls and yanked out a cop beefcake calendar. "Why don't you do something like this?" she asked, holding it up for me to see and then flipping it over and ogling the back.

I picked up my own copy and ogled the back too.

"I mean, with undertakers," she clarified. "It would be so much more interesting than cops or firemen."

"I like March," I said after careful inspection.

"You would," she replied, in her usual breezy manner. "Too muscular for me. But Mr. October could arrest me all day long."

"Oh, gross," I said.

We both laughed.

"Seriously Ken, I think people would buy it just out of sheer curiosity, or at the very least as a joke for their friends. When confronted with a choice, cop"—she held up the cop calendar with one hand—"or undertaker"—she held up an imaginary calendar with her other hand like she was the lady of justice with the scales. She weighed both calendars and pantomimed the imaginary calendar being far heavier. "See? No contest. The undertaker calendar will win every time."

I rolled my eyes. "Either put that back or buy it. I thought we were going to get a frappé."

At this point the guy who was running the kiosk zeroed his eagle eye on Keegan because she had gotten really loud and animated. "Undertaker," she mouthed to me in an exaggerated way as she slid the cop calendar back into its wire rack.

"Ugh!" I said exasperated, and grabbed her by the hand. "Come on."

Later that evening, we stopped for happy hour at Martuni's—for martinis—and Keegan brought up the calendar again, and spitballed a half dozen ideas for the calendar before switching to some juicy local gossip. I absentmindedly doodled on my cocktail napkin a calendar cover. It was a (stick figure rendition of a) dozen men holding a casket the old-fashioned way—with ropes—over an open grave. When I picked up the tab, I just stuffed the napkin into my jacket pocket with the receipt and forgot about the calendar...for a few days.

Keegan knew what she was doing, because even though I tried to fight the thought and put it out of my head, I couldn't. It just kept popping up, refusing to be ignored. Keegan had planted the seed at the mall and watered it at Martuni's. What began as a struck match quickly turned into a five-alarm fire. On the long drive back to Long Beach I made up my mind that I was going to create a calendar.

I got somewhere around Paso Robles and called Keegan.

"Ken, did you leave something?" she asked, puzzled. I had only left several hours prior.

I didn't waste time with salutations. "I'm going to do a calendar!" I declared.

She paused for a moment and then began laughing. It was the type of belly laugh I hadn't heard since before her illness. When she was able to compose herself, she said, "You're serious?"

I was amped. "I am!"

"That's classic. I'm waiting with bated breath."

When we hung up, and after I had driven a few more miles

and calmed down, it hit me: I had no *idea* how to put together a calendar.

A prudent man would've done a little research on how to logistically and financially put together a project of this magnitude, not to mention perhaps look for a distributor or at the very *least* test the winds.

But I threw caution to the wind and jumped in, in my usual manner—with reckless abandon.

CHAPTER 5

The Calendar

T he idea behind a nonprofit branched from the same idea to create the calendar, and it was crystallized on that same long ride from San Francisco to Long Beach, though its genesis was my neighbor, Natalie. Ever since my best friend had gotten ill, I had become more in tune with other people's illnesses. I found out some months before my sojourn to San Francisco that Natalie had been diagnosed with breast cancer. I knew from Keegan's experiences that battling a life-threatening illness is an extremely scary thing. Natalie was single like me, and I could only imagine that compounding things.

The day before I left for San Francisco Natalie knocked on my door. She is a pretty woman, usually very well put together, but that day she looked disheveled. "You'll never believe what happened," she said after we greeted each other.

"Try me," I said, twirling the ends of a necktie.

"My washing machine just broke."

"Oh no!" I said, cinching the knot.

She wiped a sweaty strand of hair off her forehead. She was one of those lucky ones whose hair doesn't fall out after chemotherapy. "Yeah, I've been bailing soapy water out of the tub for an hour, and it's hot as hell in my house because the air conditioner broke a couple of days ago."

What she didn't say, but I could deduce from prior conversations about her having to cut back on her hours as a legal secretary because of her treatments, was that she couldn't afford to fix the AC.

"Could I finish the load in yours?"

"You don't even have to ask," I said, stepping aside. "Help yourself. I have to head over to the mortuary. Just let yourself out when you're done."

The idea of Natalie's washing machine and air conditioner was rattling around in my brain on the ride back to Long Beach. But how could I turn that into a cause?

I liked the idea of a breast-cancer foundation for several reasons aside from the obvious ones. It has a whole month of awareness devoted to it that would be great for promotional purposes. Also, people like specific causes. I thought an ambiguous "cancer" foundation wasn't exciting enough. Yes, people like baseball, but they *root* for their team.

I figured Natalie's situation was pretty common: woman gets sick, has to undergo time-consuming and expensive treatments, has to cut back on work, starts on a slippery financial slope. The solution, I figured, was a foundation that could help women battling breast cancer in a very real, tangible way. A foundation whose sole purpose was to give gifts of money that the women could spend on groceries, child care, home upkeep, or any of the other myriad expenses in life. It seemed like the perfect solution to a real need, and it was a concept I could grasp on to, not some ethereal research charity where you're not quite sure where the dollars are going or what exactly is done with them. Don't get me wrong, those charities are all very important. Cancer research and treatment probably wouldn't be where it is today without them. But I saw a special need and decided I could fill it.

It was simple connecting the calendar idea with the nonprofit idea. The calendar would fund the foundation. By the time I pulled into my driveway at the conclusion of my San Francisco journey, I had made some big decisions.

I was going to make a beefcake calendar.

I was going to use said calendar to fund my yet-to-be-formed breast-cancer foundation.

All I had to do was execute.

I went online that very night and printed out the paperwork required to start a nonprofit. The paperwork was *inches* thick. I remember hefting the sheaf of papers and dropping it onto my desk. It made an audible *thump*. I'm no lawyer; paperwork doesn't turn me on. Just looking at it made my head hurt. Articles of incorporation, trust indenture, California required bylaws, ... there seemed to be endless facets to setting up a nonprofit.

I was in way over my head and knew it. The following day I went to see a lawyer to help me. I remember sitting in her richly paneled office and hearing her rattling off all the things that needed to be done to the tune of $500 an hour. Just *listening* to her tell me what needed to be done made my head hurt. The project seemed too daunting. I didn't need to pay someone to tell me how much needed to be done.

That evening I ran into Natalie while walking my dog.

"How was your trip?" she asked.

I told her, strangely downplaying my friend's condition as if it might diminish the gravity of hers. And I told her about my ideas for the calendar and foundation, finishing with, "I don't know, though. I met with a lawyer today and the paperwork to set this thing up seems like too much."

She shook her head and flashed a smile. "Where do you come up with these ideas? What a shame about all the bureaucratic red tape. That's a crazy idea. I'd buy one, hell; I'd buy one for everyone I knew if the guys were hot."

After the pep talk from Natalie I decided to give it another shot.

The next day on a whim I got in touch with a lawyer whom I had buried for.

"Sure, I'll give you a hand," Dana said when I told her what I wanted to do. "It sounds like an interesting idea. But on one condition—"

My heart sank. "What?"

"I get a complimentary copy of the calendar."

"Done!"

I went to her office and she pretty much set the whole thing up from her laptop while I waited, getting me a tax identification number, business license, and the whole nine yards. I'm just glad she helped me, because everything—KAMM Cares, the calendar, the book, and the TV show—wouldn't exist if it weren't for Dana wading through that mound of paperwork for me.

At one point Dana looked up from her laptop. "What do you want to call this five-oh-one-C-three?" she asked, referring to the tax code, 501(c)(3), for a nonprofit.

I had given some serious thought to this over the past week, and said, "KAMM Cares."

She furrowed her brow. "Huh?"

"KAMM Cares."

"Spell it."

I could hear the puzzled tone, so I explained, "K-A-M-M. It's the initials of my best friend growing up in Nevada City, and for whom the inspiration for this charity came, Keegan Ann Mary MacCahill."

"Okay." A few minutes later Dana said, "You're ready to go."

I was the proud new father of a nonprofit.

In order to qualify for a KAMM Cares grant, applying women need only submit a letter from their attending physician, a photo that can be used for media purposes, and a letter of hardship. I try to fill every application, and the *only* time an application doesn't get filled is if there isn't any money in the foundation coffers to give out.

The first fund-raiser for KAMM was the famous (and infamous) calendar: "Men of Mortuaries."

The advertisement in the 2005 *National Yellow Book of Funeral Directors* (now called the *Funeral Home & Crematory Directory*) read:

McKenzie Mortuaries Services announces
Men *of* Mortuaries Calendar
The deadline is fast approaching. Submit your entry for a chance to be featured in this one-of-a-kind calendar.
All proceeds will go to benefit breast-cancer research.

The press release that accompanied the ad offered a thousand-dollar prize to each selected entrant as a carrot and carried with it a $250 entrance fee to try to weed out nonserious entrants. My thinking at the time was: *Let me see if there is even interest to do a calendar like this before I go to all the other trouble.*

Turns out there was interest.

I got countless calls and emails from funeral directors all over the country wanting to know exactly what I was trying to do. Most of the correspondence had the underpinnings of disapproval, but I'm not one who is easily dissuaded. I described my grand vision to the curious, but for every ten to fifteen inquiries I received I probably only got one entry. After eight weeks I had received twenty-two entries.

About half the entrants looked like what I like to call "typical" funeral directors: guys that had never stepped foot inside a gym in their life. And isn't that what the public perceives us to be? There are certain professions that, when mentioned, the mental image of someone good-looking pops into your head. Actor, weatherman, fireman all pop into mind; funeral director doesn't. I was looking to shake up that stereotype and offer up modern, mainstream, handsome funeral directors. Of the twenty-two entrants, I selected eleven for the calendar, plus myself to make twelve. (I would like to add that I'm not so big of a narcissist that I automatically included myself as a model. My secretary, Sandee, nominated me after looking at all the contestants.) Twelve months in the year. Twelve guys. Perfect.

Well, not so perfect. At this point I had done *nothing* to prepare except recruit entrants and promise them money. Now I had to figure out how to put together a calendar.

The first order of business was to draw up storyboards for how I wanted each month to look. I sketched these out to the best of my ability and sent them to a professional artist to draw. I identified and interviewed photographers and graphic artists whose job it would be to assemble the "raw" photographs from the photographer into the actual calendar. There were also a thousand other small details like finding a makeup artist, gathering and coordinating the props that would be needed for each shot, coordinating room and board and transportation for the models, bidding the job out to printers, et cetera. And of course I had to figure out where we were going to shoot this calendar. I did a lot of location scouting, finally settling on an old cemetery called Sunnyside where the outside shots would take place. The inside shots would be done in my mortuary.

The models all flew into LAX on a Friday evening, and by Saturday morning we were onsite at Sunnyside. I borrowed an RV from a friend, almost like the kind of trailer that movie stars have on set. The RV served as a portable wardrobe and makeup station. The first shot attempted that morning was what was going to be the iconic cover, the cover I doodled on the cocktail napkin at Martuni's, with all the guys standing around a graveside, some holding lowering ropes and others holding shovels. In retrospect, we should've started with the individual shots to get everyone warmed up, and then tried for the most complicated shot. But, no, I decided to go for broke right out of the gate.

It was an absolute nightmare getting everyone looking in the same direction.

Bert, the photographer, kept shouting and clicking his hand above his head, "Guys! Guys! Everyone look here!"

It is amazingly difficult to get twelve people in sync for a precise group shot such as this one, or so I was finding out. The sun was blazing down, and it seemed like an eternity before Bert was finally satisfied. At that point I had no idea what pose we'd pick, and frankly I didn't care. I was getting a little cranky, because I was in over my head and overwhelmed by the way things were going. We were already behind schedule.

Did I mention I had no experience with calendars, modeling, photography, or the like? I knew one thing up to that point: funerals. That's it. Out of ignorance, I had my storyboards but not a clear idea of who I wanted where. So once we got the cover shot out of the way, I just started plugging models into different shots. *Inefficient* is not a word that adequately describes this method. We'd try five different guys in one shot, just hoping something would work out. It was a very laborious, inefficient way to shoot a calendar, but I didn't know what else to do other than to stick to my plan. And thus went the disorganized twelve-hour shoot.

The following day we took the remaining interior shots in the mortuary in the morning and the guys flew out in the evening. It was all over in one crazy, whirlwind weekend.

I'm the impatient type and I think I called Bert every day for the next week until he got me the photos. I was very excited, and opened the disc and began to click through the proofs.

My attitude quickly changed.

When I finished, I went back through them again. And again. And then I sat at my computer and said quietly to myself, "Shit."

I thought of all the money I had already laid out. I had put my personal finances in serious jeopardy by fronting the cash for the calendar. *Serious* jeopardy. And looking at the photos all I could think was: *there has got to be something I can do.*

My gut instincts are rarely wrong, but just to cover all my bases, I got together with the graphic artist, Dave, who was going to be putting together the calendar to have a second set of eyes on the photos.

Though I could've emailed him the proofs and waited for his reply, I needed immediate satisfaction. So I dropped everything, hopped in my car, and rode over to his house and threw the disc down in front of him.

"What do you think?" I demanded after he had carefully browsed through them twice in his usual, organized, efficient way.

He hooked a finger on his glasses and dragged them halfway down his nose so he could peer at me over them. "I think you're right, Ken. These two," he said pointing to two guys on the cover, "don't photograph well."

"What do we do now?" I asked, nearly hysterical.

"You could leave them the way they are. Just proceed."

"No," I said, shaking my head. "For this to work, I need it to be as close to perfect as I can make it." I corrected myself: "It needs to be perfect."

"You could do a different cover—"

"No," I said, cutting him off, "This is the cover I want!" I know I sounded petulant, but the project was unraveling before my very eyes.

"Can you reshoot it?" he asked, his tone never changing, though I was in hysterics.

My heart fluttered at the thought of the cost of reshooting the cover. "No," I gasped. "I simply can't . . . afford it."

"I *could* try to Photoshop it," he said, drawing the sentence out like he didn't really want to, but would if it were a last resort.

"Really?"

"Ken," he warned, pushing his glasses back up the bridge of his nose, "it may not come out the way you are envisioning, and it's going to take me some time."

I could read between the lines: *It's going to cost you.* It couldn't cost more than what reshooting the cover would cost me. "That's fine. Do it!" I said.

"I'll do my best," he said in a cautionary tone that made no promises.

I was grasping at straws and knew it, but this was a life vest to a drowning man. "I know you'll do fabulous!" I said, hoping against hope he would be.

I put out the word to the ten models I was keeping to let me know if they had any decent-looking undertaker friends.

In the meantime, Dave called me with an idea to save on cost. "Let's Photoshop Marty's head onto Matthew's body," he suggested. Marty had originally been behind the headstone. He photographed well; Matthew had not.

"Then what will you do?"

"I'll put scenery behind the headstone."

"How will that save me money?"

"It'll cut down on the number of people you'll need to fly out to reshoot. Granted, you'll only be left with eleven, but we can put an alternate shot of the cover as the month of January as kind of an introduction."

I told Dave to proceed with the suggestion.

Dave Fisch, Mr. August, came through with the model plea. He found me a replacement from his hometown, Josh Fidler. I flew Josh from Remsen, Iowa, to Long Beach where we shot "Burial at Sea," in which Josh is handing a woman a bronze urn. We shot that scene at the Long Beach Yacht Club. A passing cop stopped at the sight of the growing crowd. The lighting and screens and other photography accoutrements had drawn passersby, thinking something "Hollywood" was going on. I had to explain to the officer we were shooting a scene for a calendar. "What, the cop calendar?" he asked, confused.

"No, the mortician calendar."

He just shook his head and walked away.

The following day, we used my front yard as a "green screen" with the thought that it would best replicate the light from Sunnyside Cemetery. Using the proofs as a rough guide as how Josh should stand, Bert shot him with his arms positioned like he was holding a rope. The idea was to just edit him right into the cover shot. I was keeping my fingers crossed, hoping Dave could deliver on his promise.

After four long weeks Dave finally emailed the proofs over. I opened them with no small amount of trepidation. After quickly browsing through them, I looked through them again, this time slower. Dave had pulled it off!

I forwarded the calendar files to Keegan right away and called her. "Open your email!" I demanded when she picked up.

"Why?"

"Just do it." I waited in silence for what felt like the longest time before she began to laugh. I heard her laughing harder than she had laughed in a long time—since before her illness. "What? Is it bad?" I asked. "It's not supposed to be ha-ha funny like that."

"No, no," she said through her laughter, "it's just that I never thought you'd pull it off. Not like this. This is," she searched for the right word, "perfect. You certainly have those coppers beat."

The "Men of Mortuaries" calendar was ready to go to press.

Then I settled back and did something I'm not very good at: waiting.

The printer, a Chinese company, told me the calendars would arrive to me in giant wooden crates. The day before the calendars were set to arrive I sent Roger, an employee and model in the calendar, to an equipment rental company to rent a forklift for the following day. The plan was to drive all the crates right into the garage with the forklift. It was supposed to be easy.

You can imagine my surprise and anger when I showed up at the mortuary in the morning to find a literal pile of calendars in my parking lot. The delivery truck had arrived during the night and just pushed 55,000 calendars out the back and driven off.

The calendars had, at one point, been in cardboard boxes, but a lot of the boxes were ripped open, spilling their contents everywhere. And even the ones that weren't ripped couldn't be lifted with my rented forklift; they were too small. The mountain of calendars was a problem in and of itself, but the bigger problem was the fact there was a big, high-profile funeral scheduled to start in three hours.

I got on my phone with all my staff, waking some up, shouting excitedly, "All hands on deck! Get over here and help me move this stuff into the garage!"

It's Long Beach, so it's usually hot, and this day was no exception. I was a sweaty mess by the time we moved the last calendar into the garage, but we got it done moments before the family pulled in. There was no time to shower. I walked over to them, literally mopping my brow with a paper towel, saying, "Can I have your keys so I can pull your vehicle into the procession line?"

I hired a publicist, Jesse, to put together creative press releases and generate a buzz about the calendar. He put word out on the wire with catchy phrases to get the media interested in the calendar. "Hunky morticians; Morticians strip for calendar; Funeral directors bare all for a good cause—"

The wire worked.

There was an explosion of media attention: print, radio, and TV. Not only was the calendar a novel item, but the fact that it was benefiting a breast-cancer foundation with a unique mission made it an overnight phenomenon. So much so that New York started calling with such interest that Dave Fisch, Roger Santos, Kurt and Justin Zabor, and myself did a media tour in New York City.

I'm just a farm boy from rural California who chose the humble trade of caring for the dead. I had only left California a few times in my life, and the only time I had been to the East Coast had been to vacation in Florida with the blue-hairs. It was amazing flying to the Big Apple for the first time and being shuttled from radio to TV appearances in a limousine. We were something of minor celebrities, or at least we felt that way. The experience spoiled me. I've been back and the experience wasn't quite as dramatic.

We did Whoopi Goldberg's radio show, *Wake Up with Whoopi*. She took a special interest in the calendar because not only is she from the same neck of the woods as me, the West Coast, San Diego specifically, but she used to work as a mortician in her former life. She was really great in person. I always have an idea of how a celebrity is in person, and I figured Whoopi would be bubbly and cheerful, the persona she exudes in her movies, and she was that and so much more. I am really grateful to her for championing the calendar.

After Whoopi's show we did two talk shows and two news shows, and the following day a photograph of the four of us standing under the Letterman marquee was on the front cover of the *Daily News*.

My stupid little doodlings on a napkin in a bar had turned into front-page news on a major New York publication. I had exceeded even my own grandiose (and sometimes delusional) expectations with this project.

Jesse and I timed the publicity related to the release of the "Men of Mortuaries" calendar to coincide with October, Breast Cancer Awareness month. And after the New York trip, McKenzie Mortuary became more of a shipping warehouse than a mortuary. I wasn't prepared for the storm that came. The orders *poured* in.

I received a great deal of feedback, most good, some bad, and some outlandish (like wanting full nudity). The comments got my brain stew bubbling again. I'm not one to rest on my laurels, mainly because my ADHD won't allow it. With the first calendar I had been somewhat conservative: subjects portrayed in or around a "mortuary" setting—or some aspect of the job. I had wanted to remain respectful while also drawing some humor into the subject matter. For the next calendar I wanted to get more risqué, and show more skin (certainly not full nudity), but how? It would be impossible to remain in a mortuary setting and show more skin in good taste. How could I meet those objectives, bare more skin and remain tasteful?

Right before the last of the calendars went out the door (just in time for Christmas), the solution hit me. What did all the models of the first calendar have in common? Hobbies outside their jobs! I'd do a calendar revolving around how a funeral director spends his spare time.

That's when my accountant told me there wouldn't be another calendar.

I had poured a lot of my personal money and the mortuary's money (essentially my equity) into the calendar in order to get it going, and the way the foundation was set up I couldn't just skim money off the top to repay myself. My accountant told me I simply didn't have the finances to put together another calendar. It had been quite the expensive endeavor, much, much more expensive than I had originally planned. And to be totally honest, I didn't think there was any way I could top myself. The amount of calendars sold, and publicity generated, just seemed like an insurmountable task to surpass in the future . . . and it was so much *work*.

But I operate under the motto of striking when the iron is hot, and there was a lot of good momentum going from the calendar sales. People kept asking me, "Ken, when is the next calendar coming out?" It was simply amazing to me the amount of people that knew about the calendar. People would simply drop by the mortuary to pick up a copy of the calendar, or accost me while I was on the street or in a restaurant. If the universe was telling me anything, it was telling me the iron was red hot. So I decided to ignore my accountant's advice, throw caution to the wind, and gear up for another calendar.

I ran more casting calls in trade journals that January. And the entrants started trickling in. That was the most fun part for me, getting the mail while the entrants were coming in. It was like a mini-Christmas every day. I never knew what to expect in the mailbox. When I opened the application, I knew immediately whether they were going to make the cut or not.

In total there were thirty-four responses. Some of them I think—I hope—were jokes. They looked like stereotypical funeral directors: big guts, lots of flab, and pasty skin that had never been touched by sunshine. There was an entrance fee of a $250 donation to KAMM Cares to be considered. I thought the fee would cut down on the pranksters, and I'm sure it did significantly. But for some people cost is no obstacle in the name of a good joke. Out of the thirty-four I selected fifteen guys.

Unlike the previous year where I had twelve guys for the same number of months, I wanted to avoid the problems of people who didn't photograph well, so I made the 2008 calendar a contest of sorts. Not only did it give me some wiggle room, but it was more of an incentive for the guys to get in shape. The guys that were in the best shape and photographed the best would make the cut.

On their applications the entrants had to list several hobbies. The plan was to photograph each entrant doing two of their hobbies, that way I could pick the twelve and then whittle the pictures down further from there, depending on how they photographed.

That year I also chose applicants based on their geography. For the 2007 calendar, it had been mostly guys from California or the Midwest. I specifically targeted several East Coast and Southern mortuary schools, trying to have an evenly balanced ratio of guys from all over the U.S. I was successful and was able to recruit a very good cross-section of models from all over the country.

My reasoning behind that was simple: better exposure. If

these guys were each promoting the calendar in their specific areas, it would have a better chance of taking off and selling uniformly throughout the country. I found that in the first year the calendar sold best in California (shocker) where we were able to garner steady publicity for it. Of course, there was a real uptick in sales in New York when we promoted it there, but those booming sales dwindled after a couple of weeks. Once I had my models selected, and the theme, I just needed to figure out where to shoot it.

In real estate dealings there is the saying about the three most important aspects of a property: location, location, location! I scoped a great location, the Coast Long Beach Hotel, as the site where we'd shoot the calendar. It had a pool, fountain, tennis and basketball courts, a dock, and landscaping that could pass for a golf course, a giant grassy area for the horse to graze, a large parking lot to accommodate a collector's cars, as well as a giant indoor conference room where I had a green screen installed for any indoor shots. This would minimize the running around. I knew that if I had tried to shoot on a bunch of different sites— like an actual golf course and at a tennis club—it would be a logistical disaster and take weeks to shoot. I had learned a few hard lessons from the first calendar, and I vowed to myself that I would minimize those errors for this next calendar. This one single location meant we could, hopefully, condense the all photo shoots into two days.

Aesthetically, the second calendar turned out better than the first one. It's because I listened to the feedback and gave the people what they wanted, more skin. The final product looks a lot more comfortable, having moved away from that mortuary setting. The whole look of the second calendar is more organic than the first one, and crisper—I had finally perfected that mall kiosk calendar look.

Even with the continued success of the second edition, I couldn't continue the calendar without a distributor. I nearly bankrupted myself, twice, in the production of the calendars, and honestly, I am still financially recovering from them, but the biggest issue is time. I'm a funeral director, not a calendar publisher. The scheduling, sales, shipping, publicity, and myriad of other small details that go into this type of project were taking *hundreds* of hours of my time and my business was suffering.

I have some great ideas for future editions should a publisher come forward and want to buy the idea. Unfortunately, that's the only way I'll do a future calendar, if I don't have to do any of the legwork. I had a production company in Great Britain courting me to do a show around the making of a calendar, but I'm not going to do another one just to get on TV; my TV disasters will be mentioned in a later chapter.

But for all the financial ruin and gray hairs, the calendar has come back to me in a lot of intrinsic ways. You can't put a price tag on creating goodwill in the community like that, and it has opened a lot of doors. This book (or the previous one) wouldn't exist without it—that's how I met Todd. And it's amazing when I talk to someone and the subject comes up—people invariably have heard of "that mortician's calendar."

CHAPTER 6

10-Carat Anniversary

A centennial—a hundred years, or symbolically, ten carats. When what is now my family's funeral home opened in 1911, air flight was new technology, Ford was just beginning to revolutionize the auto industry, the Great War hadn't yet been fought, electricity had only been around for about eighteen years and wasn't yet available in many residential homes, and in the City of Wilmington—where I live—the streets wouldn't be paved for another three years.

Imagine having lived for a century and all the technological advances you'd have seen during your lifetime: personal computers, space travel, and television would be a few of the biggies that come to mind. I know there are a handful of citizens that this year will get their congratulatory letter signed by the president for their hundredth birthday. But how do you celebrate an anniversary equally as auspicious? I searched around online and found that the "standard" gift (ostensibly for a hundred-year wedding anniversary if there is such an animal) is a 10-carat diamond.

We celebrated our centennial in 2011.

One hundred years of burying the people of my community.

But we didn't celebrate with a million-dollar diamond, but rather by modifying the business name. The name of the past century, McCrery Funeral Homes, was changed to McCrery & Harra Funeral Homes and Crematory to reflect the new owner-ship of the business; my uncle, a thirty-year employee of the Mc-Crery family, purchased the business.

So what?

What's in a name?

In this profession, everything.

But really, who cares?

Obviously, the name of a business will usually tell you what kind of business it is, but it seems to me that these days most companies would rather operate under some amorphous corpo-rate name. Just ride up the main drag in Anywhere, USA, and see for yourself. Is it that nobody wants to personally back what they're peddling, or that our society has just gotten comfortable with big-box, chain-store everything? Gone are the days (in my neck of the woods) of Philip Wood's Drug Store, Storms' Shoes, and Ginther's Cigar Shop. Even our own little beloved Delaware drugstore chain Happy Harry's was gobbled up and spit out as the omnipresent Walgreens.

When I think about it, the only people who hang their name out on a shingle anymore are lawyers, the occasional car dealer, the biggie here in Delaware—a name everyone recognizes, DuPont—and of course, funeral homes.

That name on the sign is the stamp of guarantee, per se; it's the face I'd want to see when I walk through the front door of any busi-ness, especially a business that is taking charge of the earthly re-mains of Mom, Dad, Grandmom...but, hey, maybe that's just me.

Not only did the name change reflect the ownership shift, but it also reflects the changing tastes of the consumer.

...and Crematory

The popularity of cremation is on the rise in the U.S., and the percentage can vary wildly region to region. For instance, in California, where Ken is, the cremation rate is 56 percent. In Delaware, where I live, the percentage is somewhat less, 42 percent.[*] The states along the Eastern Megalopolis, as well as the ones located in the Bible belt, tend to be a bit more traditional in their burial customs, hence the disparity. No matter where a funeral director practices his profession in the future, he will only see that percentage rise. In general terms: the funeral establishment has to adapt to the times to survive. Who knows what the next big trend will be; alkaline hydrolysis (using chemicals to reduce remains to nothing) has caused quite the stir in Ohio recently.

When Albert J. McCrery Sr. started his business in 1911 out of his house on Twenty-fourth Street in Wilmington, hearses were horse drawn, graves were dug by hand, vaults were bricked out by masons, wakes were generally held in the home, and notification of death was made directly to his door, by messenger— phones were still a novelty item for the wealthy.

Things are a little different now.

Families expect a high degree of technology in the service, such as DVD slideshows and webcasting; obituaries are almost exclusively emailed; funeral arrangements are no longer made by pen and paper, but on laptops and tablets; and with smart phones the families can get ahold of a funeral director anytime of day or night by email, texting, or even good old-fashioned calling.

[*]Based on 2010 data from the Cremation Association of North America.

After *MC:USTD* came out, we continued to collect a number of interesting stories, and we came across two that are essentially the same issue but at different ends of the twentieth century. It goes to prove that each generation brings about its own advances, but also its own set of issues. So here is our centennial continuum—10-carat stories:

Runaway Hearse
Contributed by a knockaround photog

As the son of an undertaker, I had probably been to more funerals before the age of ten than most people go to their entire lives. It never bothered me, being around the dead, however, my earliest memory of a funeral happens to be the most traumatic. It was the first funeral I ever helped my father on, and he came out of the church to find me in the street, crying. Of course, I was only five years old. I was crying because I had lost the hearse.

I grew up in Oakland in the early twenties. Looking back, it was a setting out of a Steinbeck novel—all that was happening on the West Coast right after what was then called the Great War. It sure is different now. Back then it was just outlaws and characters, but I didn't really notice. I was a kid. I lived in my grandparents' house, which was the neighborhood funeral home. My grandfather set out west during the gold rush and failed to find gold, but stumbled upon his new vocation. He had apprenticed as furniture upholsterer in New York. When he was starving in some boomtown he had the bright idea of lining coffins, and the town's undertaker was born. He soon got sick of mining towns and moved farther west to Oakland, which at the time I don't think was *much* of a step up from a mining town. Even famed author Gertrude Stein felt the same way, having been quoted saying, "The trouble with Oakland is that when you get there, there isn't any there there."

Growing up in a family of undertakers, I didn't have a choice as to my career. As a child I swept up in front of the funeral home and mucked out the horse stalls. And as soon as I was able—maybe I was nine or ten years old—I was enlisted to help carry wagonloads of chairs into people's homes for wakes, and to help my father maneuver the cooling board and corpse cooler into the house to keep the body cool until the wake. And, with my father and grandfather standing at the bedroom door wiping their hands on their handkerchiefs, down the stairs I'd go carrying giant glass jars of blood for dumping in the outhouse. Back then, people were embalmed in their beds by a method called gravity injection, which is basically like hanging an IV bag, except instead of a bag it was glass jar, and letting gravity do the work. From an early age I was groomed for this profession. Even my mother and grandmother helped out in the family business. They cooked.

The bereaved family always ate a funeral dinner with us. Oftentimes there would be twenty or more people sitting around our dining room table, the men wearing weepers on their arms. A weeper is a strip of cloth worn around the bicep, the color white for the death of women and children and black for men, and until I was much older I didn't realize a weeper *wasn't* a common article of clothing. I was so used to seeing them. After dinner the men would move the table so there would be additional standing space for the wake. So, growing up, I was never shy because I was exposed to a lot of different people at almost every meal, but back then, like other kids, I was expected to be seen, not heard. I learned at an early age to speak only when spoken to.

The first time I realized I had a different home life than the other kids my age was when Lew, one of my neighborhood chums, asked me, "What are those curtains?" He was referring to the black drapes my grandmother placed over all the mirrors in the house during a wake. The thought had never crossed my mind and I told him I didn't know, and didn't he have them at his house? "No," Lew informed me, "nobody but you does."

I asked my father about the drapes and he told me it was to ensure that the only soul that was taken to heaven was that of the deceased's and not someone who happened to be looking in the mirror at the time. I don't really know the origin of that mythology, but I have also heard that it is to prevent the spirit from looking in the mirror and scaring itself because it realizes it is dead and that prevents it from reaching heaven. Either way, I haven't seen that done in at least eighty years; I guess we aren't as concerned with the soul being scared these days.

My father and grandfather left the house on the morning of a funeral wearing their cloaks—or as we called them, dooles—and black top hats. I would always run to the livery stable where we kept the horses and hearse and watch them hitch up the team, white horses if it was a woman or child's funeral, or black if it was a man's—same color designation as the weepers. Then I would chase the hearse back to the house on foot and watch the men load the casket into it.

It was about a month before my sixth birthday, I remember because I had been reminding my father for weeks how I was about to turn six and therefore would be old enough "help" on a funeral. I was itching to see where they went and what they did when they hitched up a team and went off in the hearse. My grandfather was a very stern man, and would tell my father whenever I begged within earshot that "a funeral is no place for a boy." And my father, though stern, was somewhat softer than my grandfather, who was made of stone. Finally one day I wore my father down—I dared not ask my grandfather—and he said, "Pop, this boy is going to come up in this business. He needs to start somewhere." And that was that. I was in! I was so excited I could hardly sleep that night knowing the next morning I would get to go with my father.

The morning of my big debut I blasted through my porridge and anxiously waited on the curb for the men dressed in my Sunday best. I didn't have a doole, but being the town undertaker's son, I did have a black topcoat. When my father and grandfather finally emerged, stoic expressions on their faces, I followed them to the stable and watched as they hitched their black team up, Percy and Plucky. Their fingers worked the buckles and leather straps expertly, like their fingers had a memory of their own. Finished, they climbed up by way of the buckboard and my father reached down and pulled me up onto the bench with them. I was thrilled. For the first time I rode back to our town house on the hearse, not chasing it.

While they loaded the casket I remained on the hearse. I had never seen anything quite as beautiful. It was a Crane & Breed Processional Hearse, the finest funeral vehicle you could buy at the turn of the century, made of black lacquered wood with glass windows draped with fine draperies. There were gold lanterns and gilded paint and tassels adorning the carriage; it was a piece of art. Up to that point in my life I had yet to see a motorized hearse. Things were slow reaching the west coast.

I got lost as my grandfather navigated the team through the city streets. He sat ramrod straight, occasionally flicking his whip at one of the team he deemed to be slacking and urging them on with calls and clucking. We drove far away from my house. But I did recognize when we passed the area where we hailed the ferry to San Francisco. Grandfather pulled the hearse up in front a stone church with a wooden-shingled bell tower and a lot of steps. A group of men, slouching and smoking, waited for us and they shouldered the casket and carried it up the stairs.

"Herbie, you stay out here and keep watch over the hearse," my father said with a pat on the top of the head.

"Okay, sir," I replied.

"You stay *outside*, you hear me?" grandfather said, pointing a crooked finger at me.

I gulped and nodded vigorously.

"Do a good job," father said and tousled my hair and then disappeared after my grandfather into the church.

I was eager to do a good job and be part of the team, but quickly grew bored standing next to the horses as people streamed into the church. The horses stood stock still, hardly blinking an eye. They were used to long days at a hitching post. I decided they didn't need as close watching as my father had let on.

I set off down the block looking for some children to play with, and, upon finding none, explored the block a bit. There was nothing interesting. I returned to my post hoping to find the congregation letting out, and some action, but nothing. The horses appeared not to have moved a muscle and the street was quiet. I wanted badly to go peek into church and see what was happening in there, but I dared not anger my grandfather. I tossed some stones down the street. Then I set my sights on a milliner's sign across the street.

Ping, ping, ping, went my stones as I dialed in on my target, spraying the gutter and shutters of surrounding homes.

Thwack! Thwack! Two direct hits. This unsettled Percy. He began to snort and paw at the ground. Percy's vision was mostly blocked by his blinders but he heard the direct hits and he didn't like it one little bit. His unease spread quickly to Plucky, the larger of the two. As soon as I saw my little game was causing unrest I stopped.

It was too late.

Percy and Plucky were draft horses, significantly larger and more powerful than most breeds, and they began tossing their heads, and rearing. I ran over to soothe them, but fell back in fear of being crushed as they both reared up and snapped the rotted hitching post. Free, they began ambling down the street, dragging the hitching post and hearse with them. I ran down the street and grabbed the bridle and dug my heels in. A fifty-pound boy of five is no match for two workhorses. I was jerked off my feet and dragged in the dirt street. "Percy! Plucky! Stop!" I yelled in my little-boy voice, hammering my hand against their bellies, trying to get them to stop. They ignored me and kept going, and turned down a perpendicular street. I stood at the cross street, looking back at the church and the disappearing horses, deciding. There wasn't a soul in sight to help me. I was alone. With a cry of frustration I turned and walked slowly back to the church. I had been given one job to do and I had failed!

Knowing not what to do I sat on the church steps and waited. As the gravity of my failure began to well up in me, I began to cry. *I had lost the hearse!*

Soon the bell began to toll. The church doors swung open, and the casket, borne on the shoulders of black-clad men, navigated out. They bumped to a stop, puzzled. There was no hearse to place their charge in, instead there was me, sitting on the steps, crying. My father appeared from behind the casket. "Herbie," he said, "where's the hearse?"

"I lost it," I wailed.

"You what?" my grandfather shouted.

"The horses ran off!"

If looks could kill I would've been dead, buried, and long forgotten about at that moment, but luckily, at that moment, a man came riding up the street at breakneck speed with the hearse. Percy and Plucky were going at a gallop. At the last moment, he hauled in the reigns, and the hearse skidded to a stop in a great cloud of dust.

"Mister," the man said to my father, "I've been driving all over looking for the owner of this. It appears as if they snapped the post they were tied to," he said, referring to the long wooden post still attached to the team. The man hopped down to the applause of the mourners.

My father thanked the savior and we assembled the cortège for the short walk to the cemetery without any further mishaps.

I wasn't punished, much to my surprise. My father merely asked me later, "Why didn't you follow the horses?"

"I didn't know what to do," I said as earnestly as a five-year-old boy can. "I couldn't stop them from leaving. They were too strong. So I thought to wait and tell you what happened."

"Why didn't you come in and tell me the horses were escaping?"

"Grandfather said to wait outside."

My father appeared to be taken aback somewhat, and I didn't realize why until many years later. When I was five, I viewed the world as black and white. It wasn't until I was much older that I realized the world is a very gray place. Rules sometime have to be bent in order to survive. That day with the runaway hearse turned out to be a very important lesson for me during my career, though it would be several years before I was invited to join my father and grandfather again on a funeral.

Missing Apprentice
Contributed by a guitar picker

"Jimmy!" I shouted.

The sudden noise startled the redheaded form hunched over the computer screen. I won't lie and say I didn't take a modicum of pleasure from seeing him jump.

"Uh, yeah, Pete?" Jimmy said, swiveling away from his computer.

"You're going with me today on the Scobey service. Get the hearse loaded up with flower stands and pull it around and we'll load the casket."

He stood. "Yes, sir!"

"Damnit, Jimmy, I told you this isn't the military. Stop calling me sir."

"Yes—er, Pete."

I thought for a minute he would salute, but he didn't. Jimmy grabbed his suit jacket off the chair and raced out of the office we shared. "And Jimmy," I called.

He skidded back into the office.

"Grab the casket raincoat."

"Okay," he said in a tone that told me he had no idea where the raincoat was.

"It's in the wheel well," I offered

"Gotcha," he said and disappeared.

I smiled nefariously. I secretly enjoyed terrorizing the new apprentice. He made it too easy. Loud noises, sudden movements, and dark rooms spooked him. In my defense I was just trying to bone him up. The boy had a lot to learn.

Jimmy was just out of mortuary college, and barely looked old enough to grow facial hair. He had learned all the book knowledge, but had a ways to go before he could be released into the wild. And I had the distinct pleasure of conferring the knowledge onto young Jimmy.

We loaded the casket and I said to him, "Take the hearse over to Calvary Methodist. When you get there set up the flowers and wait for me. I'll meet you over there. You know where it is?"

He stared at me; he wasn't from Nashville.

"Can I follow you?"

"No. I have a stop to make," I said and gave him directions. The stop I had to make was at the Krispy Kreme to get coffee. I didn't want to go wheeling into the parking lot in a hearse with Mrs. Scobey in the back.

I made my stop and sat in the parking lot and drank the coffee while reading the sports scores and took my sweet time getting to Calvary. When I pulled up in front of Calvary Jimmy was waiting under an umbrella on the curb. He had *that* look on his face. Though I haven't worked with him for that long a time, I know that it's the look he gets when he's done something wrong. I didn't ask, just waited for him to tell me what he had done. He always did; poor boy can't keep a secret.

We unloaded the casket in a hurry, but I still got soaked, and wheeled it into the sanctuary. I was thrilled with the way Jimmy had set the flowers up. "Nice job," I complimented.

He beamed.

They were exactly as I would've done them. *He does listen,* I thought to myself.

"Jimmy, can you go set up the guest registry and put out the service bulletins?" I asked.

"Already done sir—Pete!"

"Okay, you can go outside and begin to line the family cars up as they arrive. Here." I handed him the family car list.

He disappeared and I touched up Mrs. Scobey's makeup

before the family arrived. Lighting in churches is different than the lighting in the funeral home, so I always carry a makeup kit with me to make the changes necessary for the different lighting scenarios. I was glad it was such a dark and drizzly day because Calvary has these large windows lining the sanctuary, that, on a sunny day, make the bodies look, well, dead.

It wasn't too long before Mr. Scobey, a rotund, florid old gentleman, and his two daughters and their husbands wandered in, followed by a gaggle of assorted grandchildren dressed uncomfortably in their Sunday finest. "Pete, my boy!" Mr. Scobey said and clapped me on the back. His back slap nearly took the wind out of me. In his younger days, he could've easily knocked me over. "Everything looks wonderful. Grace looks . . . peaceful."

It appeared as if he had barely glanced at his wife arranged in the front of the church they had been attending for over a half a century, but I merely said, "Glad you're pleased, sir."

I directed everyone as to where they would be standing and what they'd be doing and asked if there were any questions. One of the sons-in-laws said, "Pallbearers?"

"At the end of the service Reverend Giles will lead us down the aisle and the family will follow. When we get back there"—I pointed to the narthex of the church—"I'll motion for the pallbearers to step from the congregation." To answer the question I knew what rattling around in his mind, I added, "The aisles here are too narrow for us all to fit."

He nodded.

"Everyone know what they're doing?"

They collectively nodded.

I left them up front in the receiving line and went to the rear of the church to greet guests. Things were going fine until a woman walked in and said, "I'm going to the cemetery. Do you have one of those little flag things for me?"

She was referring to the little magnetic flags that say "funeral" we stick on people's roofs that are processing to the cemetery. "There's a gentleman outside handing them out. You must've missed him," I said.

"I didn't see anyone out there," she persisted.

I smiled. "Don't worry. I'll get you a flag after the service. There will be plenty of time before we head to the cemetery."

She smiled brightly. "Oh. Okay."

After she signed the registry and went into the sanctuary I peeked outside. There behind the hearse were the family cars lined up with their little bright orange flags on the roofs, but I couldn't see Jimmy anywhere. I didn't want to go out in the rain, so I didn't look any farther than the protection the front porch provided. The church had a large side lot; I figured he must be lurking over there.

A few minutes later I peeked outside again. No Jimmy. I waited until there was a lull in the crowd, grabbed an umbrella, and did a lap around the church, soaking my wingtips. Still no Jimmy.

I began to get a little upset. I know standing out parking cars in the rain isn't very glamorous, in fact, it sucks, but I had served my time doing that sort of thing. It was his time to earn his stripes. I walked around inside the church and did a thorough job looking around the church hall where the post-funeral luncheon was to take place. I thought for sure I'd find him hiding out eating lemon pound cake and chocolate chip cookies. But he wasn't there either.

My fury mounted as I ushered the family up to the casket to say their last good-byes and close the casket, normally a two-man operation. Instead, I did it before a packed house as gracefully as I could manage solo. *What is he thinking,* I thought, red-faced, as I stomped down the aisle. *I am going to raise absolute hell with him. He's going to be taking night call every night for the rest of his life.* Vengeful thoughts like this swirled through my head as I stood in the narthex and watched the Reverend Giles deliver the service.

At some point anger gave way to worry. *What if he's sick?* I thought and hurried off to conduct a search of the restrooms, sure I'd find Jimmy in his death throes in one of the stalls. After investigating both men's rooms and the handicapped unisex there wasn't even a whisper of Jimmy. It was like he disappeared into thin air. I returned forlornly to the narthex just hoping Jimmy would show up.

I began to conjure up these fantastic scenarios, and I had convinced myself Jimmy had been abducted, possibly by people with ties to al-Qaeda, when Reverend Giles issued his benediction, signaling the service was over.

I trooped up front and turned the casket, and not being able to push and steer at the same time said, "Pallbearers." The pallbearers stepped out of their pews, confused looks on their faces because of the contradictory instructions I had given earlier. I swore to myself Jimmy better have been abducted by terrorists or I was going to kill him. I hate looking foolish.

I motioned to Reverend Giles. "Okay, gentlemen, here we go," I muttered, and as the assembled congregation belted out "The Old Rugged Cross" I pushed that casket down the aisle just like I had planned it.

The pallbearers got their raincoats, and I put the casket raincoat on, which is really just a fitted piece of clear plastic, and I had them lift the casket and carry it down the front walk. The congregation crowded onto the porch to watch the somber little procession, Reverend Giles leading the way, make its way across the front lawn in the steady drizzle.

At the curb, I stepped in front of the casket and swung the hearse door open. A shock of red hair popped out of the darkness.

I about jumped out of my skin because Jimmy's appearance was so unexpected, but managed to retain a look of absolute calm.

"Uh, hey guys, just doing a little cleaning up back here," was all Jimmy said as he scrambled out of the back of the hearse.

"Place the casket on the rollers," I instructed like nothing was amiss, though several of the pallbearers glanced at me with peculiar looks.

When the pallbearers had departed from the rear of the hearse Reverend Giles squared up with me. He's one of those straightlaced, old-school Methodist ministers who wouldn't say *shit* if he had a mouthful. "What the hell was that?" he asked, his usual dour expression twisted.

"I . . . don't . . . know," I said slowly.

As the last cars left the cemetery after the service was over, I walked over to Jimmy, who stood next to the casketed bier, and posed the same question Reverend Giles had posed to me.

His pale face flushed red, matching his hair, and he tugged at his collar. "I, ah, locked the keys in the hearse when I arrived at Calvary. And then later, when I was out in the parking lot and nobody was looking, I crawled through the backdoor and fished the keys out of the ignition with a coat hanger I found in the church's coatroom."

There is a little viewing window that separates the rear of the hearse from the cabin that he must've used to access the cabin from the back.

"That's when I realized I was trapped," Jimmy continued.

"None of the doors in the rear of the hearse have an inside handle."

I wanted to laugh, but I kept a straight face. "I know," I said stoically. "Generally, people don't need to let themselves out of the *rear.*"

"I saw you walking around out there and I was pounding on the windows, but you had your head down." Jimmy must've equated my straight face to anger, because he repeated. "Pounded!"

I thought of my wet wingtips.

"I called you about fifteen times," he said. "You never answered."

I checked my phone. I keep it on silent by force of habit. Sure enough, there were nineteen missed calls.

In a small voice he said, "Am I going to get fired?"

I finally let a laugh out. "No, of course not. But you're going to have to work on your fibs a little better. 'Just doing a little cleaning back here' was the best you could come up with?"

It's a big jump to go from hearses that are drawn by horses to ones that have electronic brains smart enough to lock themselves on their own in only eighty years. We have at the funeral home a ledger from 1912 that shows Albert McCrery conducted business with my great-great-grandfather Isaac, shipping a body via "Pennsy" (the nickname for The Pennsylvania Railroad) that runs the length of Delaware. Now we'd just drive the scant sixty miles. Technology is certainly changing things, making some things easier, but as the previous stories demonstrated each generation brings about its own set of solutions and problems.

Most people champion the ease technology brings into our lives, but it is a double-edged sword. For one, the funeral professional (like a lot of other professionals) is now reachable and on call 24/7 thanks to the advent of cell phones. Yes, times are changing for the better or worse, but there is one thing that isn't likely to change. Unlike a lot of other industries that are outsourcing to China, my business is one that will be guaranteed to be around for the next hundred years, our bicentennial.

CHAPTER 7

My Television Failures and Hollywood Calling

'm always looking to do something different, something to push the envelope. So, when a production company contacted me about doing a spot on my mortuary for the Swedish television show *Outsiders,* or *Utomstående,* I was thrilled.

McKenzie Mortuary. On TV! Isn't that every American's dream? To be on television?

Even though it was for a foreign television program, my excitement wasn't dampened in the least.

Needless to say, I couldn't say yes fast enough, with the hasty caveat that they make a donation to KAMM Cares.

The production company, Titan Television, scheduled the host and a film crew to come to the mortuary, which coincidentally overlapped with the arrival of the models for the 2008 calendar. The film crew was very excited with all the goings-on having to do with the calendar. They wrongly assumed my normal, day-to-day life was filled with the hubbub associated with the calendar production. The crew followed me around and filmed everything I did for three days, but the show wasn't about the calendar, it was about what I do on a day-to-day basis, so most of what they shot wound up on the cutting room floor.

What Titan Television conveyed to me that they wanted to capture was the process I call "bedside to graveside," which is essentially the process from the time-of-death to when the casket gets lowered into the ground. A family I'll call the Smith family gave me permission to include them as part of *Outsiders*. The crew filmed me making the funeral arrangements with the family, embalming Mrs. Smith (they filmed me, not the decedent), dressing and cosmetizing the remains, as well as working the funeral service. Since Mrs. Smith was going to be cremated, there was no burial aspect to the service, thus no dramatic cemetery shots.

The film crew wasn't really anything paparazzi like it might sound; it was just a sound guy and camera operator and good-looking hostess, named Anna, tagging along after me for a few days asking questions in broken English, some of which didn't make too much sense. I really struggled with the language barrier.

Really, the whole thing was painless. I expected them to want to do multiple takes and all that, but it was a lot like I envisioned reality television to be filmed—one continuous stream of film.

I wish I had asked more questions, but I was so blinded by the fact that I was going to be on television I just cruised along with the whole process. I agreed, I signed their papers, and I let them film and ask their questions.

I was furious when the show aired.

Actually, to be more precise, the show had already aired when I finally received my copy in the mail—nine months later. I'm not sure if that was intentional or not because they knew how angry I'd be and try to cancel my spot.

In everything I do—the calendar, the estate sales, the foundation, the toy drives—I do it all to further the cause of the profession I love and have devoted my life to, but also to change perceptions. People, I think, for the most part view funeral directors as pariahs and opportunists. Jessica Mitford's scathing exposé, *The American Way of Death and Dying*, does a good job of summing up all that negativity. I want to shatter those stereotypes, and that is why I was so upset with *Outsiders*. It just reinforced to me what people think of us, and goes 180 degrees against what I'm trying to do.

Outsiders, which airs on Sweden's *Kanal 5*, is essentially a documentary show. I (wrongly) thought it would be an educational-type documentary of how Americans funeralize their dead. Not so. The tag line describing my episode* reads, *"jobben som ingen vill ha"* which translates to, "the jobs that nobody wants." I didn't sign up to do an episode about jobs nobody wants! I happen to love my job.

The best way I can describe the episode is as the American equivalent of *Dirty Jobs*, starring Mike Rowe. In *Dirty Jobs*, Mike does unsavory, dangerous, or literally dirty jobs. This show did the same: giving an exposé on "dirty" jobs. There were two other jobs featured in the episode besides mine: a woman cleaning out Porta Potties and two men cleaning out hoarders' houses, essentially trash.

I couldn't understand a word they were saying, but I sure got the gist of things when they show me in my mortuary, and cut away to a woman literally vacuuming shit up.

What does this convey to the viewer when the dead are sandwiched between excrement and trash?

---

*Season 7, episode 5.

It's easy to see how these reality stars get stuck in a moment. It's their fifteen minutes. The sun is shining upon them, and their fifteen minutes turns into something that haunts them for the rest of their lives, all in the name of almighty TV.

I was upset, but it aired in Sweden, so really, who cares? Really, the reason I was upset was the fact that I felt like I was duped. And it was like pulling teeth to get them to fulfill their contractual obligation to donate to KAMM Cares. I got this song and dance about the problems associated with converting kronas to dollars, but after I continued to pester them they relented. I felt like saying to them, "You basically tricked me, the least you can do is make your obligatory donation to a nonprofit without a fuss."

The next time I was able to wrangle myself into a television gig I was a lot more careful.

Apparently, I wasn't careful enough.

A producer named Kevin called me from a production company we'll call "Nameless Productions." Logo TV had a show called *The Arrangement* in which a pool of ten florists compete for the title of America's Best Floral Designer. Kevin had an idea involving Omarosa Manigault for an episode.

For those of you who don't know who Omarosa Manigault, simply known as Omarosa, is: she made her big splash on TV in 2004 on Donald Trump's show *The Apprentice*. She gained notoriety on the show as a "bad girl" because of her behavior and furthered it by a controversial appearance on *The Oprah Winfrey Show*. Since then she has appeared on several other shows. Her shtick is being controversial. The producers of *The Arrangement* had the bright idea that one of the challenges would be to design a funereal floral tribute for a mock funeral for Omarosa.

Kevin Googled "mortuary" and our first book, *MC:USTD*,

popped up, so he called me and pitched me the idea. Omarosa is such a villain on TV, they thought it'd be cute, and make a lot of people happy, to watch her "funeral." Nameless Productions wanted me to be a guest judge. They figured a funeral director would be able to offer a more practiced eye for a funereal piece than the regular judges.

"Sounds like a great idea!" I said after listening to his whole pitch. I had a great thought. "Where are you getting the casket?"

Silence. "Uh, I haven't gotten that far," Kevin admitted.

If you haven't noticed, I'm always angling to promote one of my causes, so counterpitched Kevin this deal: "I'd be happy to donate one if you'd showcase the book, and the fact that part of the proceeds go to raise money for my breast-cancer foundation." The episode Kevin was pitching me was set to air in October, Breast Cancer Awareness Month, and I had visions of cross promotions floating in my head.

"I read that on the website. That's a great idea," he said, jazzed by the fact he was getting his guest judge and casket with a single phone call. "Uh," he interjected, deciding to push his luck, "Would you be able to provide three caskets?"

"Sure," I said without hesitation.

"Oh, this is really great! We'll do a screen shot of your book before the credits, and introduce you as funeral director *and* author."

"Funeral director and author," I echoed. I liked the sound of that: *author*. Makes me sound distinguished.

We exchanged emails, and then I got off the phone and called my publicist at the time and got him to email a high-resolution PDF file of the book cover to Kevin. Next, I called my casket representative at York and told him about the idea for *The Arrangement*. He was pretty excited, in the reserved way that only a casket salesman can get. Casket manufacturers like to see their product featured on the big or little screen.

I directed my rep when and where to deliver the caskets. I had three similar caskets delivered, all 18-gauge carbon steel caskets, but in different colors: black, bronze, and a silvery gray. Kevin wanted a couple different colored caskets so he could figure out which one worked best in the studio lighting.

And then I called Todd to brag about the TV spot I had landed our book.

A month later, wearing a freshly dry-cleaned suit, sporting a freshly trimmed haircut, and wearing my breast-cancer-pink tie and a matching lapel ribbon, I found myself in studio.

"You'll be attending the funeral of a famous personality," Gigi Levangie Grazer, hostess and judge of *The Arrangement,* said to the remaining six contestants to begin their funereal challenge. She revealed the funeral would be for the personality of Omarosa. Then she had the contestants race off to make corsages (that one would ostensibly wear when attending a funeral).

After the little corsage challenge, which Omarosa judged solo, Gigi challenged the contestants to make a "coffin saddle." It is a little pet peeve of mine when caskets, which have *four* sides (plus a top and bottom), are called coffins, which have *six* sides. Coffins haven't been traditionally used in America for about a hundred and fifty years. Every once in a while I come across one, but it's rare. In other parts of the world, however, coffins are still commonplace. During a newscast when I hear the word *coffin,* I can let it go, but I cringed when the word *coffin* flew out of her mouth, because I had donated three *caskets,* and I, the resident expert, was sitting right there and should've corrected her. But I was scared to incur the ire of the director so I kept my gob shut.

During the coffin-saddle challenge, with thirty minutes left on the clock, the contestants were given the added burden of making a standing spray of flowers to compliment their coffin saddle, but using, of all things, silk flowers. Tacky. I felt bad for the contestants, because every once in a blue moon someone will send a silk arrangement to a visitation and silk flowers look awful next to the real deal, no matter how quality they are. The contestants, to their credit, did an admirable job of putting silk arrangements together that looked pretty passable.

In addition to Gigi, on the judging panel was Eric Buterbaugh with Omarosa and myself guest judging. I have a lot to say about everything in general, but when it comes to my passion and profession, funeral directing, I tend to be outspoken. Needless to say, during our seven-and-a-half-hour taping session (that was just for the funeral segment of the show) I ran my mouth non-stop about the contestants' floral pieces. That's what Kevin wanted me for, right? My professional opinion?

Really, they were all great pieces, really inspired, and interesting, but Kevin wanted me for my expertise, so I commented on both the positive and negative aspects from a professional's eye. What looks good might not necessarily work at an actual funeral or wake. You can imagine my dismay when I watched the show and my sound bites were cut down to somewhere around forty-seven seconds.

And, aside from the introduction, there was no mention of the book name, the foundation, nor was there the promised screen shot of the cover.

Todd called me right after the show aired. "Ken, I thought there was going be some mention of the book."

"Not only that," I said, feeling immensely foolish, "but there was supposed to be a screen shot of the cover."

"What happened?"

"I have no idea," I replied.

I'd been duped, once again.

I was furious, but the bell had already been rung, and I couldn't un-ring it, so I called Kevin worked up in a lather and demanded a contribution be made to KAMM Cares as a consolation.

No contribution was ever made.

Looking back, it's my fault for being so trusting and not getting anything in writing. Technically, Nameless Productions weren't contractually obligated to show that screen shot or mention my breast-cancer foundation in the credits, but dummy me thought that if I donated my time and three caskets (as well as a church truck), then our verbal agreement would be honored. I've lived in LA long enough to know the City of Angels can eat you alive—it's worlds away from Nevada City where a man's word is contract enough. I guess this just proves I'm still a hayseed at heart.

However, from that mess sprang an idea. I'd been kicking around the idea of doing a television show for a number of years. With the launch of the first book, and the good publicity that it was generating, it suddenly seemed like the right time to try my own show. Like everything else I do, I didn't bother to test the waters first. I just jumped in.

I hired a cameraman and had him shoot a sizzle reel, which is essentially a short film about the gist of what the show will be about—in effect a calling card. My amateur sizzle reel is pretty awful. I like the *idea* of being on camera, but I need to brush up a little on my anchorman-type on-camera poise. That became painfully obvious as I watched three and a half minutes of me giving a tour of the mortuary and greeting people coming in for a memorial service. To be fair, I hired the cameraman on the cheap and the camera work and editing were pretty awful.

Even so, I believed I had a product that could fill a void out there in TV Land, so I trotted it out to a few production companies, one of which signed me to a contract. Unfortunately, because of the terms of the contract, I can't write about my show, but in general, broad strokes: Once a production company has signed you they will budget a certain amount, usually around sixty to seventy thousand dollars to shoot a (real) sizzle reel, which is then used to entice a network to sign your show. Once a network signs the show, then the pilot episode is shot and it either takes off or flops. And the rest, as they say, is history.

Maybe I'll make it, or maybe I'll end up entombed in some unseen film vault like many, many people with dreams of the big and small screen.

I don't hold much stock in self-acclaim, but I do in results. I've learned in business that all it takes to get results are two things: ambition and courage. That's it. Easy, right? No, it's not *easy*, in that respect as nothing worthwhile ever is, but it certainly is a lot easier than living with the regret. A lot of people are too fearful, or too timid, or too worried about what everyone else will think to take the first step to realize their dreams. Confucius said, "A journey of a thousand miles begins with a single step." I don't think he was necessarily referring to physical distance travel.

I'm living proof that you don't need a ton of talent to realize your dreams, just a tiny bit of ambition and some courage. I came from a family of modest means, and started a business in a community where I saw a need. I had to cut through a lot of red tape and really fight for that business to get it started. Even though I ate ramen noodles many nights, business is . . . busy. Todd will attest to the fact that I'm not very good at stringing a sentence together on paper; I now have several books out, and though it damn near financially ruined me, and I have never been on the cover of *GQ*, I've been in a calendar—twice. And even though my sizzle reel is rough, I've decided I will make a go of television. Who knows what's next.

The point is: if you have an idea you think will work, go for it. Make it work. If you dwell on the reasons why it won't work, or will fail, then it will. You'll self-fulfill your own prophecy. Don't wait for Hollywood to come calling, call on it.

CHAPTER 8

Cremation and the Goat

 touched on this in the "10-Carat Anniversary" chapter, and it will most likely be the bulk of the business by the time I retire—cremation.*

It's the new way to funeralize someone... or so seems popular opinion.

To quote the Bible, Ecclesiastes to be specific, "What has been will be again, what has been done will be done again; there is nothing new under the sun." Cremation has been around for thousands of years; early man found it a convenient way to get rid of decomposing remains that would've otherwise caused disease. The Greeks are the first civilization credited with "inventing" the practice, and it was commonly used until the Middle Ages when the Christian Rite associated it with paganism and

---

*The first reported cremation in the United States was that of Revolutionary War colonel Henry Laurens. Colonel Laurens chose cremation because he was terrified of being buried alive after his daughter was mispronounced dead and almost met with that fate.

banned it. Even the early Romans engaged in cremation practices until their conversion to Christianity.

In America, cremation is growing in popularity* as Christianity has begrudgingly accepted it as an acceptable form of disposition. In other parts of the world, where other religions are the majority (such as Hinduism and Buddhism), cremation has remained the preferred form of disposition. Regardless of the religious history of the practice of burning a human body, it is definitely gaining popularity with mainstream America and there's no denying it, like some might argue global warming isn't happening. According to the NFDA the cremation rate rose 11 percent nationally in ten years (from 1999 to 2009). That's an average of 1.1 percent per year. CANA (Cremation Association of North America) reported in 2013 the annual growth from 2007 to 2012 was 1.85 percent per year. And I expect the reports are for more aggressive growth into the undetermined future. Too bad my 401(k) doesn't boast that kind of growth.

Change isn't bad, it's just hard. Especially in a profession that is so staid and mired in religion and tradition as this one is. It's going to be painful for some, but those firms that persevere over the next half century will have to have changed. It's a fact of the business, just as sure as the sun rising in the East in the morning. In the future, the "modern" funeral director will be part memorial planner, part techie (because the memorial services will be based on technology), and part cremationist.

Just so we're all on the same page I'll define some funereal terms. A memorial service is a funeral rite in which there is no body present, and a funeral service is a funeral rite in which the

---

*CANA reported in 2013 a national average cremation rate of 42.0 percent. It is predicted to be at 49.1 percent by 2017.

body is present. Hence, after somebody has been cremated you'd have a *memorial* service for him or her.

As to *why* cremation is gaining such popularity, your guess is as good as mine. I don't think there's any singular reason, but there are most certainly a combination of reasons that people choose it.

Some people argue because it's cheaper than a traditional burial. Yes, cremation *can* be less expensive, but not necessarily. It would be like me saying, "Buying an apartment is cheaper than buying a single-family home." In most cases that statement would be reasonably accurate. But, like anything else in life, it depends on choices. If I chose to buy a five-hundred-square-foot apartment in Manhattan it's going to cost me a lot more that buying a five-thousand-square-foot mansion in, well, anywhere. But an apartment anywhere other than Manhattan is probably going to cost less than a single-family home.

It all comes back to choices.

If you're simply cremating the remains and taking the cremains—we say *cremains*, not *ashes*, because it sounds nicer—home, then it probably will be less expensive because you're saving on the services and rental casket and cemetery costs. It's the same as buying a car with fewer options: it's going to be inherently cheaper because you are purchasing less. But if you funeralize a person in a "traditional" way, meaning the community pays their respects to the body, the body gets cremated, and then the cremains get buried in a cemetery, then a cremation versus a casketed burial has a negligible price difference. And yes, in reference to the last sentence, cremains can get buried in a cemetery just like a traditional burial. In fact, unless someone has other plans for the cremains, I recommend it.

The thing I worry about when people take cremains home is

their *ultimate* disposition (in the eyes of the law, cremation is final disposition, hence the reason it is legal for someone to take the cremains home). What happens when a hundred years from now Jane Doe's great-great-grandniece's husband is cleaning out the basement and pulls out an unmarked urn, blows the dust off it, and gives it a puzzled look (and maybe a shake to determine the contents) and then yells, "Hon, what the hell is this?"

"Oh," Jane Doe's great-great-grandniece says, taking the urn from her husband's hands and cocking her head, "I think my mother told me this is my great-grandmother's cousin, who she called Sissy Mitt."

"Do we have to keep them?" the husband asks.

That's no way to treat someone's remains no matter how long they've been dead!

When in doubt: bury them, scatter them, make them part of a coral reef, or shoot them to the moon. But do something with them!

Another reason people choose cremation is because it's more earth friendly than burial—or at least that's what I hear. I'm not going to argue the point with someone who already has their mind made up, but the fact remains that retorts use *a lot* of fuel during the cremation process. A retort—the name for the actual combustion chamber—can run off of a number of different fuels including natural gas, liquid propane, or diesel. A natural gas burning unit is going to burn somewhere to the tune of two million BTUs an hour (and possibly more if the state requires a preheat burner in the unit). To break it down: a retort is going to use roughly the amount of natural gas it would take to heat the average-sized single family home during winter for *two* weeks for *one* cremation, about thirty to forty cubic feet of fuel.

But on the flip side, they don't pollute. A modern unit will emit less pollution particulate matter in a month than an average fast-food restaurant chimney will emit in a day.

And finally, there's the ease of it all. It used to be that when someone died the undertaker would come to the home or apartment and embalm the remains (in the deceased's bed), and then the undertaker's minion would bring a load of folding chairs into the house for the wake and funeral. There was a movement out of the house and into the funeral home for the wake and service, and now it seems as if there is a movement to do away with the guest of honor. Would you have a wedding without the bride and groom?

Granted, it's less emotional to have a service without the deceased present. But grief isn't supposed to easy. It's supposed to be messy, and emotional, and tough. It's okay to cry at a funeral; in fact, it's normal.

We're a society based on convenience. In our drive-through-coffee-shop-nation, death doesn't always fit into our plans. So, without a body waiting around to be viewed a memorial service can be pushed off for weeks, months ... or years.

That being said, I think I'd like to be cremated.

I like the idea of the versatility of the cremains, and how the deceased can "live on" in more than one place than in an impersonal cemetery that generally has no connection to the deceased's life. When our family dog Boomer died, we had him cremated and scattered his ashes in the woods behind our house where he loved to run, and in the ocean where he spent countless hours chasing his tennis ball. I know he's "only a dog," but for the other pet owners, you know how they become a member of the family. So now when my current dog is splashing through the surf in a single-minded mission of retrieving her ball, I think about Boomer. In scattering his ashes in the ocean, the ocean has become a living memorial to him.

A higher profile example would be when country singer Tim McGraw sprinkled the ashes of his father, Tug McGraw, onto the mound at Citizen's Bank Park when he threw out the ceremonial first pitch in October of 2008. Tug was a relief pitcher for the Philadelphia Phillies, the one who got the last out when the Phillies won the Series in 1980 (which for us Philadelphia fans is a big deal because we only have two Series titles).

Regardless whether one chooses cremation or burial, memorial or funeral service, when done right, it should accomplish the same thing: be a fitting final ceremony. It is the proverbial period at the end of the sentence, and the service should be predicated upon the person's life, not convenience, ease, or an economic bottom line.

The most vivid memory I have from my paternal grandfather's funeral is at the cemetery. He was a full-bird colonel and combat veteran. I can distinctly remember walking behind the caisson, holding the flag-draped casket, down one of the many tree-lined streets from the staging area to his final resting place with the brass band playing the army song and the riderless horse *clip-clopping* along. It was a beastly hot and humid day in August, and the honor guard contingent seemed to not even shed a drop of sweat, while the mourners, clad in black, flanked the yawning hole in the earth, women fanning themselves, and the men just waiting for the signal when they could all take their suit coats off.

It was fitting because he was a war hero, and now when I think of him I think of that memory, that day in Arlington. I'm glad I have that memory.

The story of the goat came to us from the Bible Belt. I like it because it illustrates how an unorthodox service can have more meaning than a regular service. And since we're on the subject of cremation...

The Goat
Contributed by a motorhead

I rarely cry at funerals. Okay, I never cry at funerals. It's my business, and as such, I have to have some level of professional detachment in order to conduct business. Therefore, I never cry at funerals. Ever. But then Sloan Prentice died, and all bets were off. Funny thing was, I didn't even know Sloan.

It was late September when Sloan Prentice died, the time of year where autumn has already encroached north of the Mason-Dixon Line but in the Carolinas the dog days of summer are still tenaciously clinging to warm weather. I'm a transplant due to marriage, originally from New Hampshire. This is the time of year when I can drive to work with the top off my Corvette, and my parents have forecasts of snow on the six o'clock news. It was a hot, humid day Sloan died with the forecast calling for rain, so I drove my pickup truck to work. The 'Vette—my baby that I rebuilt from a chassis I found in a junkyard—never makes an appearance when there's the chance of inclement weather. When I arrived at work that day my boss handed me a call sheet that had come in during the night.

"I'm going to need you to make funeral arrangements with this family," he told me.

"Sure," I said, looking at the call sheet. I noticed the deceased was a relatively young woman, mid-fifties.

An hour later a man dressed in a flannel shirt, jeans, and a John Deere cap came in. "Hello," I said. "Don Randolph."

The man, Trey, introduced himself; he had that soft southern drawl that kind of flowed slow and smooth like syrup out of a bottle.

Once we were seated in my office I said, "I'm very sorry to hear about your wife's passing."

Trey took of his cap and patted his hair self-consciously and then shrugged a little and pursed his lips. "Yeah, it's a tough knock. I'll tell you, it's going to be tough not having her around no more, but we had a good ride while it lasted." He toyed with his cap for a moment before setting it on the desktop.

His response wasn't what I was expecting to hear come out of his mouth. It was the type of philosophy I wasn't used to, practicality borne out of the lifestyle that is a little more hardscrabble than what I was used to in New Hampshire. Since I wasn't sure how to respond to him, I decided not to, and began gathering the vital statistics. As we talked Trey periodically spat into a plastic coffee cup. When I had gathered all the necessary information for the death certificate, I leaned back and asked him, "So, Mr. Prentice—"

"Trey." *Spit.*

"Excuse me?" I said almost reflexively. I was still learning the language. "Oh excuse me, yes, uh—Trey, what are we going to do to memorialize your wife?"

"You ain't going to believe this, but she had some strange wishes. Her being sick and all for a spell it gave her some time to think."

I smiled. Though I was young, I thought I had heard it all already. "Try me."

He leaned forward and told me, and as my eyes widened, he smiled a little, and spit, and then started from the beginning, as if he had to justify it to me. "My wife was born to Virgil and Betsy Davis. They lived out in the foothills over yonder toward the Ten'see border. Virgil was an auto mechanic who ran shine."

"Shine?"

Trey smiled at my naïveté and used to opportunity to spit. "Moonshine. White Lightning."

I nodded. "Oh," I said. Like I mentioned earlier, I'm a Yank. Shine is as foreign to me as a UFO.

"Anyhow," Trey continued, "Virgil was known throughout five counties for his ability to bore and stroke an engine. He souped up cars for all the other runners and had quite the business. But at night he drove too—ran the shine from the hills down here to Salem." Trey paused to spit before continuing. "He had this old '37 Ford with the flathead V8 he bored out and stroked like you wouldn't believe possible then he slapped a supercharger and a turbo on it." He stopped and laughed. "Must've been a sight; neither Sheriff nor the Feds could touch him. Old girl must've ridden like the wind."

I nodded. "I bet."

"I think, in later years, he didn't even do it for the money. He liked the thrill of the hunt. He just liked to drive. The war changed him. After he got back he still worked on cars for other guys, but stopped running shine. He still loved to drive and he got real involved in stock car racing." Trey spread his hands apart to show how big Virgil was into it. "He taught his only child, my wife, how to drive. Hell, she practically grew up on the track." Trey picked up his hat off the desk and twisted it in his hands, and bowed his head. "She was good, real good. Got the trophies to prove it," he said, softly to the carpet. "Paper clippings she's kept claims she could've been professional. She was that good.

"One day she wasn't feeling well so her daddy raced the car. It was raining that day and the track was slick. He wrecked and was killed. Sloan lost her nerve after that day. She never raced again." He looked up at me. "I never saw her race. It was before my time, but she always had a taste for fast cars. Right after we got married that's when she got her '69 Judge that I was telling you about earlier."

"Sounds like a pretty sweet car."

His face lit up. "Oh she was. Carousel red, it was Sloan's pride and joy."

"Ram Air III engine?"

He paused, and looked surprised. "You know cars?"

"A little."

Trey laughed. "Nah, it was IV, believe it or not."

I whistled. "That is one impressive Goat." Car enthusiasts, like myself, call Pontiac GTOs Goats, and The Judge is the crème de la crème of the herd.

"Yes it is, one impressive Goat. She loved that car almost as much as she loved the kids." As an afterthought he added, "And me."

"I'd imagine."

"So when can we do this?" Trey asked.

"I'll call you."

A couple of days later, after I had gotten the proper authorizations, I cremated Sloan Prentice, and her cremains were returned to me in a little plastic box about the size of a dictionary. That day I called Trey. He told me he'd be over the following day and we'd do the deed.

The weatherman called for rain, but I took my 'Vette to work that day anyway. It seemed fitting. At nine o'clock on the dot I heard Trey arrive long before the doorbell sounded. When I opened the door, there idling at the curb was an immaculate beast of a car. The bright red looked like it was covered in glass it was so shiny, and true to the beast, it idled rough, an undulating growl that kept threatening to die at the bottom of each sonic valley.

"She's as nice as you claimed."

"She's a beaut," Trey agreed.

He was wearing a different flannel, same jeans, but no cap.

"I'll get my car and meet you around front," I told him.

"Those your kids?" I saw a couple of people huddled in a Mustang Mach III behind the Goat. It was yellow with two wide green racing stripes, and the sheen was dull and matte. Compared to the Goat, it might as well have been a piece of garbage compared to a rose.

"Yeah. They aren't happy about what's about to go down."

"I bet," I said under my breath.

I pulled my 'Vette around and followed the little procession on a circuitous route that reminded me somewhat of a parade because all our cars were classics. We pulled our parade into the junkyard and Trey stopped the gleaming Goat in a clearing. I killed my engine and picked up Sloan from the passenger seat. I carried the small plastic box into the middle of the clearing. The Goat's wheels were black and glistened wetly. "I spent all night waxing her," Trey said softly and patted the roof.

It looked it.

"Where do you want me to place Sloan?" I asked, holding the urn.

"Driver's seat."

I leaned into the car. The interior appeared to be all original, and looked and smelled like it had just left the showroom floor. I placed the urn on the soft leather seat and closed the car door.

Sloan's children had gotten out of their vehicle and stood by it sullenly. They were a motley assortment of two boys and a girl all wearing the standard uniform: jeans and flannels. A toddler of maybe two or three clung to the girl and screamed. The screams were the only sounds in the junkyard. The mother did nothing to quiet the screams.

Trey bent over the hood of the car, both hands on the hood, head bowed, as if in prayer, then he backed away and yelled, "Gary!" to an unseen person. He made a twirling motion with his hand.

The six of us stood in a semicircle around the clearing while the Goat sat like a prizefighter alone in the ring. I suddenly noticed the day was cool. Autumn had arrived. The child screamed louder when a front-end loader roared into the clearing. It was yellow and new and covered with dust. It squared off with the Goat and then the machine's forks dipped under chassis. There was a hydraulic noise and the Goat got lifted up into the air and gently placed it into a niche. I grimaced because I knew what was coming next.

And it did.

There was another hydraulic noise and the walls of the niche began to compress. I could feel the beginning sting of tears in my eyes when the glass exploded. I quickly dashed them away. Trey bawled openly and the forks of the yellow beast fought to keep the Goat into the niche. Metal screeched and protested, and in the end all that was left was a Carousel Red pancake.

The walls expanded and the loader picked the flattened car out and drove it away.

We stood in silence for a minute, and Trey's children, sullen and sulky, piled back into the Mach III, revved the engine and roared off. "What now?" I asked.

"It'll be taken to be shredded," he said, not answering my immediate question, "and recycled."

"Oh."

We stood in silence for some time, both staring at the now empty niche, before Trey broke the silence. "Okay. Let's go."

We got into my car. "Nice ride," Trey said, running his hand over the dash.

We both knew he was patronizing me. My 'Vette couldn't hold a candle to the Goat.

"You're going to have to tell me how to get back. I'm totally lost," I admitted.

Trey pointed this way and that as we rode home, but mainly we rode in silence until Trey finally said, "You're probably wondering why."

"Kind of." In truth, I was—no pun intended—dying to know why.

"Sloan and I are the type of people who die like we live," he said, easing up on one cheek and pulling a tin of tobacco from his back pocket. I watched in horror as he pinched off a wad the size of a chicken's egg and stuffed it into his mouth *in my car.* "It wouldn't be honest if we got some preacher up there saying how she found Jesus right before she died. She loved the cars, the race, though she pushed it away when racing took her daddy. But it's where her heart belonged. And, I think, in some small way she can rest in peace knowing she went in a similar way her daddy did, in her car."

"But why not have a memorial service in your backyard with the car, or at the track? Why destroy her car?"

"She wanted that. She knew nobody could take as good care of that Goat as she did, especially our kids. You see that pony?"

I nodded.

"Disgraceful."

I shrugged. I had been watching his lips for even a hint of tobacco juice spilling out onto my upholstery, so far so good.

He looked at me. "Don, how do you want to be remembered?"

The question caught me off guard. "Honestly," I said, "I don't know."

Trey laughed. There wasn't any tobacco spray, I noted. "Well, I'll be. An undertaker that doesn't know how he wants to go. That's like a mechanic that doesn't have a favorite type of car." We pulled up in front of Trey's home. He got out, spit a stream of tobacco as long as a rope, wiped his mouth on his sleeve and leaned into my 'Vette. "Well let me give you a bit of advice. I'd figure it out and tell your wife. That way she's not standing there with you dead not knowing what to do. Golly, wouldn't that be ironic." He offered me a calloused hand and winked, "Me, it was tough, but I knew had to slaughter a goat in order to appease the Gods."

CHAPTER 9

The Busy Season

There are three kinds of lies: lies, damned lies, and statistics.

—MARK TWAIN

T he question I think I'm most frequently asked is, "Ken, when's your busy season?" "What am I, an accountant?" I want to respond, but who wants a glib undertaker? So I mumble my typical mix of days-getting-shorter, holidays-over, flu season mumbo jumbo, and kind of trail off, and then stand there and stare at the asker with an expression on my face that assures them I've satisfied their curiosity.

Of all the things to be inquisitive about: an undertaker's "busy season." I can think of a thousand things on my list—like, how were the Egyptian pyramids built? Is Keith Richards really still alive? and, What do they put into Cheetos to make them so damn addictive?—before I'd be interested in someone's busy season. Then again, I find most people have a morbid streak they don't like to admit to.

I think the question stems from the newspaper. Some days there are a handful of death notices, and the next day there are three pages' worth. People are curious as to why there are wild ebbs and flows. And believe me, *everyone* reads the obituaries, whether it be the old paper format or online; we're all curious as to who is dying in our community (and what they are dying from, as if you can avoid cancer, Alzheimer's, Parkinson's, car wrecks, runaway buses, lightning strikes, or falling asleep while smoking and burning the house down). Clarence Darrow, the famous lawyer, was quoted as saying, "I have never killed a man, but I have read many obituaries with great pleasure." Perhaps the pleasure comes partly from the fact that you get to say to yourself while reading the obituary, *better him than me.*

I've been in this profession now for over twenty years, long enough to collect anecdotal evidence of a "busy season." It seems to be after the first of the year. I guess it makes some sense. The holidays have passed, the days *are* shorter, and the weather *is* colder. You've made it through the holidays, one last hurrah with your loved ones. Your natural circadian rhythm is telling your body it's hibernation time because of the cold weather and dark days. Seems as good a time to pass as any...

And there is the more practical reason: people feel ill around the holidays and don't want to burden the rest of the family with their ills, so they grin and bear it, when otherwise they would've sought medical attention.

At the end of the day, who knows? Maybe one day science will definitively prove something, but until then, we'll have to stay satisfied with my half-baked guesses. Perhaps people are so damn interested in the "busy season" because they plan on avoiding the first quarter of the year as they get older. Good luck.

Though I cannot really attest with any scientific accuracy to a busy season, an experience I had recently with my mother caused me to notice the interconnectedness of us as a species in death. That's heavy, I know. Sorry to lay it on you like that. I'll try to clarify: I've observed inter-human connections manifesting in death.

I have so many examples where the husband and wife will die on the same day, or same day of a different month, or the day of some anniversary. It happens far too often for it to be non-random.

Aside from my casual observations, there is historical evidence. Take for example Aldous Huxley and C. S. Lewis, both renowned British authors (though technically Lewis was born in Ireland). Huxley and Lewis died the same day, November 22, 1963. Their deaths were overlooked, largely due to much bigger news that day—the assassination of John F. Kennedy. What are the chances of two people of the same profession from the same country (albeit a small country) with the same amount of fame dying on the same day? Small. Very small.

Have I sold you yet?

No?

Well, take the American presidents. They are a very interesting sample group when it comes to death relationships. Two of them died the *exact* same day. Thomas Jefferson and John Adams share July 4, 1826, as their death day. Which in of itself is an eerie coincidence, but add to the fact that the day they died was the semicentennial (or quinquagenary for you lexiphiles) anniversary of the signing of the Declaration of Independence, a document they both signed, makes it a little more than a coincidence, don't you think?

Of course, there are two other sets of presidents that died the same day but different years, as well as one that shares July 4. Millard Fillmore and William Taft both died on March 8, Fillmore in 1874 and Taft in 1930. And December 26 is the death date shared by Harry Truman and Gerald Ford, Truman in 1972 and Ford in 2006. James Monroe joined Jefferson and Adams in 1831.*

At the time of the writing of this book there have been forty-four presidents, five still living, meaning thirty-nine presidents have died. Three sets (two sets of two, and one set of three)—or 18 percent of the dead presidents—have shared a calendar day, one set sharing the same day *and* year. This can partially be explained by something known as the "birthday paradox." The birthday paradox is a statistical tool used to calculate the probability that a set of people will share the same birthday . . . or death day.

The chance of any two people sharing a death day is less than three-tenths of a percent, but as you enlarge the pool of possibilities the chance grows exponentially. It only takes a room of only twenty-three people for there to be a 50 percent chance that two people will share a death day. In the case of our presidents, there's an 87 percent chance that our pool of thirty-nine dead presidents, two would share a death day. But does the birthday paradox explain away that the probability of this happening dwindles to a mere 17 percent when looking at the three sets, and drops to under 1 percent when looking at Jefferson and Adams sharing the same day and year?† Add to the fact that Jefferson, Adams, and Monroe all died consecutively (the second, third, and fourth presidents to die), and it gets less and less likely their deaths aren't simply random occurrences. An independent

---

*Compared to the three sets of presidents that share death days, only one set shares a birthday. James Polk and Warren Harding were both born November 2.

† You've got to be kidding if you thought I calculated that stuff! I had a statistician lend me a hand.

probability of that date—July 4—occurring three times in a row is roughly one in fifty million, or like rolling a 4 three times in a row...on a die with 365 sides.

Coincidence?

If you think so, I have some snake oil for sale.

Statistics are all well and good, but in truth it's just a bunch of abstract gobbledygook. Really, the academics can crunch numbers to make anything look anyway they want, so I want to share my experience, and then you can decide if you believe in the nonrandomness of death or if I'm just feeding you a load of crap.

When I used to work for Lotus Chapel I was assigned to take care of a family, and that's how I met Don-of-the-Dead. Of course then he wasn't Don-of-the-Dead yet. He was just Don. Don's father had died, and he came in to make funeral arrangements with his mother. As was my usual routine I took them into the casket selection room and explained to them the differences among the different makes and models and types and then allowed them to browse in a no-pressure environment while I loitered outside the door in case they had any questions.

After about ten minutes, Don moseyed out of the selection room, leaving his mother roving between two choices, running her hand along the shirred interiors.

"I've always been interested in the funeral business," Don said.

"Oh?"

"Yeah, I often thought about it when I was a kid."

"What do you do?" I asked.

He made a quick, diminutive movement and smoothed his hair. "I work for Boeing as an accountant."

I chuckled and rolled my head around. "Kinda far removed from this."

"Oh, I know."

I glanced at his mother, and saw that there was now a third casket she was closely inspecting. "Do you have any questions?" I called in to her.

"No, Kenny, I'm fine," she said and waved her hand at me. Turning my attention to Don, I said, "So why didn't you get into the business?"

His attention was fixed on his mother. "She was a young woman during the Depression. She's a very conscientious shopper; likes to know exactly what she's buying," he said, almost to himself. Then, snapping himself out of his quasi-trance, said, "Ah, you know how it is. If you didn't grow up in the business, it seems...like...how do I get into it?"

"I didn't grow up in it," I said.

"Really?" he replied, interested.

I told him my abbreviated story; I felt as if there wasn't enough time to give him the whole saga. He seemed enraptured by it. "So, your family doesn't own this business?" he asked.

I laughed. "No." At this point in my career, I was fed up with Lotus so I ended with, "In fact, I'm thinking about leaving here and starting my own business."

"No kidding?"

"No kidding." Impulsively, I added, "If you ever decide to leave Boeing, look me up."

Don was about to reply, but at that moment his mother came to the door and said, "I think I've made a decision."

Don came back a few days after the funeral to pick up the death certificates. I wasn't busy so we went to a café and had coffee and talked about funeral service. Don kept in touch, and we became friends. Shortly after I buried his father, I started McKenzie Cremation and Burial Services.

Don took my rash offer seriously, and decided to realize his childhood dream. He took an early retirement from Boeing and took that money and bought into McKenzie Services in its burgeoning months.

Don was christened with his Don-of-the-Dead name by my best friend, Keegan. I have several friends named Don, and over the years have had several employees named Don. So one day on the phone I was yakking on about a Don, and she blurted out, "Who are you talking about, Don-of-the-Dead?"

"Don-of-the-Dead?"

"Yeah, the Don that works with you . . . and the dead," she said. "Get it?"

I laughed, "No, I'm talking about Don, my neighbor, from down the street."

"That's Downtown Don."

"Uh, right."

After that day the name stuck.

Don-of-the-Dead does all the stuff I'm incapable of doing because unlike him I don't have the Jedi mind-set and patience for mounds and mounds of paperwork. He does the taxes, keeps the books, does the payroll, and all the other business-oriented bureaucratic horseshit that I'd jump off the closest bridge if I had to deal with. Don-of-the-Dead also helps out around the mortuary in a pinch, working funerals and making airport runs and such when we're swamped. Really, he's a godsend. We're great partners, though we're polar opposites.

Don-of-the-Dead is very quiet and humble, opposed to me, who's a loud braggadocio. Whereas Don-of-the-Dead is content to mingle quietly and have meaningful conversations at a cocktail party, I'm not satisfied until I'm wearing a lampshade on my head and leading the entire crowd in a rendition of *It's Raining Men*. I think that's partly why we complement each other as business partners so well; he's the rock behind the scenes, while I'm the talking head out front. Our personalities seem to run over into this weird contest we've seem to be having (against our collective, conscious wills) that correlates with our personalities. For example (I kid you not, this is a real example), one day I pulled into work, full of myself because I had just bought a brand new Ford F-150—pipes, off-roading package, the whole nine yards. When I strolled into the mortuary, Jane, the receptionist, was talking to Don-of-the-Dead at the front desk and says, "Hey, Ken, you see Don's"—the staff doesn't call him Don-of-the-Dead—"new car? The Camry?"

"Uh, no," I stammered.

"You probably parked right next to it," he said, visibly pleased with himself. Don is the sensible type of guy who buys a new car every ten years. "It's where I always park."

"Oh, oh yeah!" I said, feigning I had seen it.

"C'mon," he said, unusually animated, "I want to show you this one really cool feature."

"Maybe a little later," I said, "I have a ton of stuff waiting for me."

"It'll only take a second," Don-of-the-Dead said, already holding the door open. "This is going to blow your mind."

"It's really cool, Ken," Jane chimed in from behind the desk.

Thanks a heap, Jane!

The parking lot at the mortuary isn't huge, so it didn't take Don-of-the-Dead more than a second to say, "Who parked in your spot?" He blinked and looked around, "Where's your car?" Don-of-the-Dead is sharp and I didn't even need to say anything before he said, "Oh."

"What is it you want to show me?" I said, trying to sound more excited than I was.

There stood Don-of-the-Dead staring at his sensible, neutral-colored sedan next to my big blue truck. "I'm sure you have the same feature on your new vehicle," he said, stalking back to the front door. Throwing it open he yelled, "Ken bought a new truck, damn it!"

"Ken," Jane scolded when I walked through the door, "couldn't you have given Don one day to have the new car?"

"What?" I said, holding my palms up. "I had no idea he was getting a new car."

She gave me a look that said *yeah, right.*

"Honest!"

That's how our little "contest" goes. I don't really know what to call it, because the word *contest* denotes we are consciously competing. Our little game is totally off the cuff. Don-of-the-Dead will come in and announce he has booked a trip to Florida, and I will have, on the previous night, just booked a trip to the Mexican Riviera. Don-of-the-Dead gets a DVD player, I get a BluRay player; Don-of-the-Dead gets a baseball autographed at a charity event, I catch a fly ball at a Dodgers game; Don-of-the-Dead puts a fountain in his backyard, I put in a pool. And then our little "contest" got really strange, really quick. It all happened in a single day, and now I'm convinced Don-of-the-Dead and I are connected on levels that the human psyche isn't conscious of.

I remember the day well because it was one of those sunny days that aren't too hot, and so crystal clear you can't believe anything could go wrong on such a day. We get a lot of sunny days in California, but this particular day, there wasn't a single cloud in the sky. As I got out of my truck in the mortuary parking lot, the sky stretched before me like a giant azure canvas. Jane greeted me, and before I went to the job board to see what tasks awaited me, I went to the break room to grab a Perrier and found Don-of-the-Dead sitting at a table just staring at a cup of coffee. This was very strange. Don-of-the-Dead is a quiet person, but he is never still. I had never, until this day, seen him take a break. He's always hunched over his desk, half-moon glasses perched on the tip of his nose, rifling through reports, or walking with purpose around the mortuary toting reams of paper.

"Who died?" I asked, yanking open the refrigerator door. I drowned out his response by saying, "Damn it! Someone stole my Perrier." I poked my head up over the door and said, "Sorry, Don, what did you say?"

"My mom."

"Your mom what?"

"Died."

"Oh my God!" I said, hurrying to the table and pulling out a seat. "I am so sorry." I really was. I absolutely adored Mrs. Donan.

"She was ninety-two; I knew it was coming, but—but still, it's . . . ," he paused, searching for the right word. "Weird."

"What are you doing here?" I asked. "Why don't you take a couple days off?"

"I couldn't sit home, all alone. I wanted to be here, where she is."

I've been working with death long enough that he need not say any more. I knew what he was trying to say. I got the glass carafe of coffee and topped off his mug and said, "Give me a little time."

He nodded. He knew what I was saying.

I left Don-of-the-Dead hunched over his coffee and headed to the preparation room. I have been preparing human remains for my entire adult life. It is second nature to me; I think I could do it with my eyes closed, but it was a strange experience. I was meticulous to the point that I was almost second-guessing myself, every step of the way. It took me most of the morning, but finally I escorted Don-of-the-Dead to the chapel, like I have so many families, where his mother lay in blissful repose.

Leaving Don-of-the-Dead in the chapel, I went upstairs and

showered and finally sat down at my desk to see what little paperwork Don-of-the-Dead had meted out when the phone rang.

"Hello?"

"Ken?" It was my sister-in-law, and she sounded a little frantic.

"Arieanne, what is it?"

"It's your mom. She just collapsed at Walgreens and they have rushed her to the hospital."

I stood. "Oh my God? What happened?"

"We don't really know. She is en route to the hospital right now. The paramedics think it may be a heart attack."

"Should I come out?" I asked. "I can leave right now." My mom lives in Arizona where my brother, Kevin, and sister-in-law live. It isn't exactly around the corner. It makes more sense to fly there, but I was prepared to run downstairs and get into my truck and start driving.

"Wait a little bit," Arieanne said. "I'll call you back in an hour, or sooner if I have some information."

I wandered downstairs and found myself sitting in the same molded black plastic seat that Don-of-the-Dead had occupied all morning. Gone was the calm, semidetached professional I had been. I was replaced with a person who didn't have a clue in the world what to do. I tried reading the newspaper, but couldn't concentrate, so finally I just sat and stared until all my emotions grew and grew until they were about to burst. I decided I needed to drive to Mesa. I had to do *something*.

Just then, someone came to the door of the break room. "Ken, phone."

I ran to the nearest desk and snatched up the blinking extension.

"Ken," Arieanne said, her voice stretching out like she was calling down a subway tunnel, "she didn't make it. Mom is dead."

Mom. Is. Dead. Three simple words. Words that I understand. Words I hear often. But on this day the words didn't really compute. I just stood there at a loss for words for the longest time and the strangest thought popped into my mind: *I'm an orphan.* I still think about having that thought, even today. I was a grown man with a career and all that stuff, and all I could think about was how I was suddenly all alone in the world in the sense that the person I had always looked to for guidance was gone.

"Ken, Ken, are you still there?" Arieanne was saying.

"Oh, oh, yeah, I am," I heard myself saying. "I'll send someone out. They'll leave now," and some other words before hanging up. I stood there in a daze and I remember standing there and someone asking me what happened, and my response.

I didn't want to go home, and I couldn't accomplish any work, so I just kind of paced aimlessly around the mortuary.

Word must've filtered through the mortuary and into the chapel where Don-of-the-Dead sat, because he found me. "Ken," he said, "I'm so sorry about your mom. Such a young woman." He didn't even ask what happened; he knew we would talk about it later.

"Thank you."

"I would be honored to drive to Mesa to get her," he said.

I put my arm around Don-of-the-Dead. Here was a man who had lost his mother some eight hours prior and was willing to set his grief aside and do something significant for someone else. The gesture brought tears to my eyes. "No, I've already sent someone. But thank you for the gesture."

"Are you going to—"

"I don't think I will be able to," I replied, knowing he was asking me if I was going to embalm my mom. "She is a donor, and I simply can't see her like that."

He nodded. Even though he wasn't a funeral director, he had

worked in the business long enough that he intuitively understood. Don-of-the-Dead took my shoulders and looked me in the eye. "When she gets back here, you call me at home. I'll come in and sit in the preparation room with her while they do their work."

I couldn't speak, only nod. I squeezed his arm to let him know how much his gesture meant to me.

It takes seven hours to drive from Long Beach to Mesa one way, and if you factor in the paperwork at the hospital and stops to gas up it was a sixteen-hour round trip. The sun was just starting to peek above the horizon when Mom arrived at the mortuary.

Based on the time it took Don-of-the-Dead to pick up the phone, he was sitting next to it waiting for it to ring. I understood; I hadn't slept either. "I'll be right over," he said.

And so, like Don-of-the-Dead had done less than twenty-four hours prior, I paced in front of the preparation room door while one of my embalmers did their labor. I've often wondered if I would be able to embalm someone with a real close degree of kinship like my mom. If it were a straight case—meaning she had died of natural causes—I don't know, and will never know. But since she was a tissue donor—a very invasive procedure—I couldn't bear to see her like that.

Being in the profession, I've often touted the benefits of viewing the body, but until I was led with trepidation toward my own chapel to view my mom, the peace it brought me is still—to this day—indescribable.

Mom had regained the dignity death had stripped from her.

As I stepped up and grasped her cool hand, I noticed there was a small smirk played across her lips. It was almost like as her last unselfish maternal gesture she was offering me a final gesture, one of solace.

That evening, both moms lay side by side in the preparation room. Lucy Donan was ninety-two, and her passing wasn't unexpected. Susan F. Cole-McKenzie was sixty-two, and her death had been very sudden. What are the chances of two business partners who own a mortuary having their mothers, of different generations, die on the exact same day, five hundred miles apart? I think I stated earlier in the chapter that I'm no statistician, but I'd venture a guess that the probability is slim. Slim enough to offer some evidence that death isn't necessarily random, and that our species is connected on different levels that we aren't aware of. Sure, Lucy and Susan met at big milestone parties and events we've had at the mortuary. They were proud of their boys. But what was their real connection, or is it my connection with Don-of-the-Dead? However I want to bend my mind around it really depends on the day and my mood, but the one thing that remains the same is the fact that the night both moms were lying next to each other in the preparation room was one of the most significant times in my life.

CHAPTER 10

Stuff Happens

I think the most oft asked question I get (in statement form) is: "Todd, your job... it's got to be depressing." I'm no psychologist, but I postulate that the asker is almost seeking to reaffirm their stereotype of the person that would *want* to work with the dead. I can see that. To the outsider it must seem like doom and gloom and death and dying and tears and crying every day, all day. But really, I find it the opposite.

I think most of my brethren would agree that it is a very uplifting job—a calling, even—in which I get to help people realize the meaning of a loved one's life. In that respect it's a big responsibility because you only get to do it once. Other occasions come around much more often, so you get time to perfect them. Birthdays and anniversaries happen every year. Marriage you can take several shots at (or more) if you are so inclined, same with baptism; sometimes it doesn't take the first time. But a funeral, you only get one chance to get it right.

I also enjoy the fact that the job is versatile. I find myself in all sorts of situations and different places every day meeting a true cross section of Americana, everyone from the homeless to the vice president of the United States (Joe Biden is from Delaware, so it's not uncommon to spy him at different local functions). That versatility is sometimes a double-edged sword. Since no two days are alike I have to constantly be ready for the unexpected.

They don't teach you this in mortuary school, but a successful funeral director is one who is able to adapt. There is a saying in the military that goes something like: plan for the worst, and hope for the best. A funeral is a social event we plan out in excruciating detail, and if everything goes according to plan then the day of the funeral there really should be nothing left to do except sit back and let the ship navigate on autopilot. But . . . even the best-laid plans go awry, and that's when your mettle gets tested. Here are several stories about what happens when things don't necessarily go according to plan.

The Houdini
Contributed by a trap shooter

I pulled a disappearing act one day at the cemetery and ever since then have been duly dubbed "Houdini." I'm not sure why. Copperfield would be more appropriate. David Copperfield is known for making things disappear. Houdini was an escape artist. But you can't pick your nickname (just look at the nicknames in the Mob); I guess Houdini has a better ring to it than Copperfield.

I don't know if the heavens ordained me to be accident-prone or if I'm just plain clumsy, but I must've been born under a bad sign. Stuff seems to happen to me . . . like that fateful day in Dogwood Hollow Memorial Park.

We pulled through the cemetery gates shortly after noon.

It had been raining pretty steadily since the evening before, and, like the pattern of most storms, the black clouds suddenly broke and it was a bright, beautiful spring day. I was driving the hearse, and followed the cemetery lead car through the maze of tree-lined drives toward Section E where Mrs. Everett was to be interred. A memorial park is a cemetery where there are no upright headstones; all the markers are flush with the ground, giving the appearance of lush, undeveloped land. I had been in Dogwood Hollow the week before and noted how the grass had really greened up during that time. Spring was definitely here.

When we arrived at the gravesite, I let Callie out to double-park the cars in the procession on the drive. I pulled the hearse into the proper stop denoted by a small mat the cemetery grounds crew had laid on the grass near the drive. The green cemetery tent stood a good clip away from the drive. "About as far as it could possibly be," I muttered, annoyed. The median age of the pallbearers was eighty, and they had struggled merely to lift Mrs. Everett into the hearse at the chapel. Now they were going to have to carry her the length of a football field.

"Pallbearers," I called, and motioned for them to step from the assembled crowd.

Six old men tottered to the rear of the hearse.

I sidled up to Callie. "I'm going to need you to help us," I whispered.

She nodded.

"Okay," I said, and gave them instructions on how to grasp the handles of the casket. Then as a caveat, added, "The grass is going to be very slippery, so *please* step with caution."

I noticed the granddaughter had a flip cam out and was filming. *Dear God, please don't let anything happen,* I prayed.

It seems these days every minute of everyday is being filmed so we have to watch not to adjust ourselves or pick our noses or whatever lest it end up on someone's funeral video of Mom or Dad, but to have one of these old men take a spill and drag down the whole casket with it would be an absolute nightmare—and Internet video sensation.

"Pastor," I said to the minister.

She nodded and began walking toward the gravesite.

I pulled the casket out, the granddaughter filming, and off we went.

I swear I was hauling at least 75 percent of the weight of the casket, but somehow we made it all the way across Section E and the slippery grass without anyone tripping.

When we got to the grave there were two cemetery men there to help place the casket on the lowering device. The lowering device sits up on supports and has a roller on the leading edge. You place the casket on the roller and pull it across the lowering straps.

I was at the head end of the casket, the first end to go onto the device. I instructed them all to step up onto the supports and pull the casket onto the device.

They did without incident.

The granddaughter kept that camera rolling.

"Okay, gentleman. Thank you," I said, standing on the device, looking at the casket resting securely on the lowering device, the hundred yards of wet cemetery ground we covered, and the six heaving old men, astonished we'd made it. "Just step off the way you stepped on and you can rejoin your families."

That's when the stuff hit the fan . . . or actually the opposite.

I stepped backward off the device and next thing I knew I was *in* the grave. Or at least I think I was. It was very dark and I had a mouthful of mud, and I couldn't move. My arms were pinned above my head.

I heard a woman scream. I tried to scream too but couldn't due to the mud in my mouth.

Strong, calloused hands grabbed my wrists. All of a sudden I felt like my arms were going to be ripped out of their sockets. I kicked feebly with my feet but to no avail, they dragged up the dirt sides of the grave like a plow furrowing a field. The burly gravediggers hauled me up like I was a rag doll and placed me on the green Astroturf mats.

There I stood, covered in mud, stunned, and facing a rolling camera.

"Jeff!" Mrs. Everett's daughter, Sue, cried. "Are you all right?"

I doubled over and retched. A small clod of dirt came flying out. "I'm fine, I'm fine," I managed to say between fits of coughing.

I waved off all other inquires about my well-being and fled to the safety of the hearse while Callie finished up.

I was covered from head to toe in runny, red mud. I doubted that the dry cleaner could salvage my suit. I dug out the piece of plastic that is called the casket raincoat and put it on the hearse seat for the ride back to the funeral home.

On the ride back Callie broached the subject. "So, Jeff, what exactly—"

I cut her off, "I don't want to talk about it."

The next day my night call partner, Carl, greeted me with a big shit-eating grin. "Hey, Houdini!"

I didn't even ask. I knew *why* I had the name. I just wish I could've been a little more like my namesake and escaped from that grave instead of having two gravediggers pull me out like they were firemen rescuing a helpless little kitten from a tree. Hell, I couldn't even move to try to salvage a scrap of dignity!

Callie later told me that it looked like I had just vanished into thin air; one minute I was there and the next I wasn't.

What happened was Dogwood Hollow had dug the grave the day before the service. The vault company had come the morning of the service and dropped the lower piece of the burial vault into the hole, and placed the supporting woodwork around the hole and then the metal lowering device on top of the woodwork. Then, to make the gravesite appear nicer, placed green Astroturf carpeting over the wood. There had been a small cave-in on one side of the grave due to the rain-loosened earth. And when I stepped backward off the wooden scaffold it was like stepping on a hole that just had a carpet laid over it—almost like a booby trap. When I dropped in my arms went up over my head like I was stepping into a plunge pool. And Callie said all they could see was my wiggling fingers sticking out of the hole.

I said before, I'm accident-prone. I've fallen (I hate to admit it) more than once down the stairs at a family's house on a removal. I've slipped on ice at night and slid right under the hearse, and even face-planted in a cemetery on a granite headstone slick from the sprinklers, to name just a few of the more illustrious arrows in my quiver, but those have mainly only been in front of Carl. Rarely have I committed one of my swan dives in front of an audience with cameras rolling.

And to think, I was worried about the elderly pallbearers.

Somewhere out there, there is quite the exciting funeral video. I cringe to think it'll ever see the light of day. Hopefully it'll stay buried in that hole I was in.

Golden Gloves
Contributed by a boxer

When I enter the room to make funeral arrangements I always get the same reaction: "You're so young! Whatever possessed you to do this?" Then they pause for a moment and ask the real question that's on their minds: "What happened to your nose?"

I'm convinced the first question is couched to segue to the second. What they really want to know is why my nose is so horribly disfigured. And the answer to both questions is the same: boxing. Boxing was my genesis, getting a kid off the mean streets in a questionable neighborhood, and it was almost my demise. I was twenty-two years old when I started to shake like I had Parkinson's and have noticeable memory loss.

Everyone I've ever talked to about my days in the ring tells me they're scared to death—literally—of being physically beaten. I was never scared in the ring. In fact it was the opposite; all the worries the world threw at me dropped and I entered a Zen place in my mind the second I stepped between those ropes. Even when there's that split second before the KO punch hits your jaw and you realize you've let one by. No, the only time in my life I've ever been fearful hasn't been in the ring. It was pulling up to a cemetery for a graveside service, forty-five minutes late, with "Mom's" casket in a pickup truck.

I was working for an outfit called Kelleher & Sons when Jane Logan died. I starting working for Paul Kelleher when I was just out of high school, making my rounds on the amateur boxing circuit with dreams of a pro card and doing removals for Paul on the side. When my body gave up on me, I went to mortuary school and Paul hired me on full-time.

Jane Logan died in late autumn, well after the first freeze. It's not an easy time in the Upper Midwest. We just muddle along and hope to make it through to spring. Thus far that year we had had it pretty easy snow-wise. The day Mrs. Logan died, I went on the removal, embalmed the body, and made the funeral arrangements.

Kerry, Jane's daughter, made the arrangements, and we scheduled the burial for a Thursday. Due to family members flying in and out it had to be Thursday. This is common this day and age for a funeral to be predicated on everybody's busy work/school/vacation schedules. Once we had the detail of the day hammered down, I asked her, "Will we be having the service at a church or here at our chapel?"

"At the grave."

I cocked my head. "Are you sure?" I asked in my nasally tone. My sinuses do a 90-degree turn and it makes me sound permanently stuffed up. "December in Minnesota can be a little cold to be having a graveside service. Not to mention dicey, weather-wise," I counseled.

"That's exactly why I'm having it outside. My brother," she rolled her eyes, "is a Pentecostal minister in Florida and if I give him a warm place to preach he'll be all day. That wasn't mom at all. This day is about mom."

I grinned at her. *Touché.*

We agreed to meet at the cemetery at ten o'clock on Thursday and have the graveside service.

I called Northlake Memorial Park with the grave order. I knew they would build a fire on the grave that would burn for a day or two to loosen the ground up enough that they could get in there with their jackhammers. That was Monday.

Wednesday night it snowed. A lot.

I phoned Kerry Thursday morning to try to talk her

out of a service that day. Due to obligations of other family members, it had to be on this day.

I acquiesced against my better judgment and hung up the phone, sealing my fate, and went to the garage to put snow chains on the hearse, loaded Mrs. Logan's cherrywood casket, and set out for Northlake. Kelleher & Sons is on the outskirts of Duluth, and the quickest way to the cemetery was through a nature preserve. Since I knew the going would be slow I wanted to take the shortest possible route. Notice I said *quickest*, not *smartest*.

The going was fine on the primary roads. We do a pretty decent job in my neck of the woods of getting plowed out reasonably fast, but once I entered the confines of the preserve I started to get a little nervous. The roads are twisty and narrow, and because of growth on either side of the road it appears that the road is just going to get swallowed up by forest.

The roads were still pretty bad in places, but I was starting to relax. It was nice and warm in the hearse, I had plenty of time to get to the cemetery, and the combined weight of the monstrous machine, the casket, and the friction of the snow chains were making for a smooth ride through the snow.

Then I came upon a plow.

I could tell it was one of those huge state-owned plows by its orange coloring. It was barreling toward me, its huge blade putting off a plume of snow like a rooster's tail. I inched the hearse as far over as I dared to give the plow maximum clearance. As we drew closer, I got nervous. The roadway had only been plowed a lane and a half—at most— and that blade was wide. I inched over again. The plow showed no signs of slowing.

I was beginning to sweat, and slowed down, considerably. As the rooster's tail came closer I saw I was going to have to get over even more. I white knuckled the hearse over as far I possibly dared and slowed her down to the pace of a man jogging. Thankfully, she held steady. Then, right before we were going to pass I saw the road was just too narrow.

I wrenched the wheel right at the last possible second and floored it. The big V-8 engine responded and roared forward. My life flashed before my eyes as the blade sliced mere inches from the window. The forward momentum suddenly stopped as the hearse came to a sickening *crunch* in a snow berm.

Shit!

I hopped out of the hearse and watched the plow disappear around a bend and get swallowed up by the frosted evergreen forest. "What the hell?" I said, quietly, almost to myself, like I couldn't believe the driver hadn't seen his plow force another driver off the road and didn't bother to stop and help. Then my blood boiled and inner-fighter reared its head, "What the hell!" I shouted and kicked the chained tire—what little was exposed of it. I was stuck up to the tops of the wheel. Sighing, I got back into the hearse. I knew it was stuck, but I was going to try to ease it out of the snow berm and continue on my merry way.

I dropped her into reverse and she inched backward slightly before the tires spun. I quickly shifted to drive and cranked the wheel. Nothing. The wheels just spun and spun. I tried forward and reverse several more times, but to no avail. I was stuck good. These were in the days before everyone and their kid had cell phones, and even now you don't get reception in the nature preserves. So calling for someone to winch me out was out of the question. It was going to be up to me.

I sighed and threw her into park. I wasn't going to get unstuck by sitting waiting for a miracle—I never won a fight by hoping my opponent would knock himself out. We keep a shovel in the equipment bay of the hearse and I retrieved it and began digging. I was only wearing my topcoat, wingtips, and calfskin gloves and a little set of ear warmers and in no time I was soaked and chilled to the bone, but I kept digging. I may as well have been trying to move a mountain, but the mantra from my fighting days—*never surrender*—ran through my head as I dug.

The fight was against Miguel Guerres. He was a former Detroit Metro Golden Glove Champ, welterweight like me. It wasn't a sponsored amateur fight. It was a backroom fight—a KO fight, basically one that goes on until someone gets clobbered. I should've known better, but it paid well and I needed the money. Miguel was fast and strong and I knew it, but I got into him early, and he was on the ropes early. And then I overreached and left myself exposed for a split second. That was all he needed and he laid a blow on my face that was like an atomic bomb to my nose. In an amateur match the ref would've stopped it for RSCH (referee stopped contact head injury), but it wasn't, and he didn't. The crowd went wild when it got a taste of blood. *Never surrender* repeated in my head as blood gushed down my face like a fountain and I flailed wildly trying to keep him at bay.

The mantra repeated in my head as I dug a trench back to the road and tried rocking myself out.

I kept repeating it in my mind as I put the car mats under the wheels and when that didn't work I muttered it under my breath as I went into the woods to break off evergreen boughs and laid them under the wheels for traction.

Nothing. It was like she was stuck in quicksand.

I got back into the cabin of the hearse to warm up. Glancing at the dash clock, I thought, *What am I going to do now?* I was frozen to the bone, and the time for the service was drawing near. I would never make it even if I freed myself that second. But what could I do? Failure was not an option. The only alternative was to keep digging. After a few precious moments of warmth I got out and picked up the shovel. I dug and dug and dug. My feet lost feeling first but still I kept digging. My fingers and hands went numb in the poorly insulated gloves and my hands kind of froze into position around the handle but still I kept digging. *Never surrender, never surrender, never—*

Blood was still trickling down my face, though my trainer had stuffed cotton up my nose, an excruciating experience. I dipped and wove, hoping to find an opportunity to end the fight as quickly as I could. I knew if I didn't end it I'd pass out. Miguel took the opportunity to stall and pepper my face with blows. Even blocking, each hit was unbearable. Fatigued, and barely conscious, I let him slip one by and scored another direct hit on my nose. I passed out.

It was my last fight.

An hour passed with no traffic before a jacked-up pickup rumbled down the road. The driver, upon seeing the hearse, slowed and rolled the window down. "You need help, fella?" he asked. He was a country boy through and through.

"Yeah," I replied.

"Watcha doing driving that thing in this snow?" he asked.

"Got a burial," I replied. I approached the battered truck. It had once been painted a shade of mint green but time and mud made it hard to discern its present color.

"In this?"

"Yup. You have a winch by any chance?"

He took off his stocking cap and scratched his head. "Nope."

"You mind giving me a lift to town so I can call a tow truck?"

"What time is your burial?"

I looked at my watch. "Right now."

"If I give you a lift to town it won't do you much good. All the tow trucks are out plowing."

"I know, but what else do you suggest I do?"

He grinned revealing three teeth that were the color of corn. "Hell, I'll take you to your burial."

I looked at him and then his truck. As if to prove its moxie the truck backfired a little. I made a fast decision. "Okay."

He lit a cigarette with a cardboard match. "You best shovel that out first." He jerked his head to the bed of his pickup, filled with snow for weight. I didn't hesitate and climbed into the bed and shoveled it out in record time while he sat and smoked.

I pounded the fender and hollered, "Clear!"

"A'ight. I'm going to back her in," he yelled and revved the engine, his voice lost in the roar. The huge three-foot chained tires backed right into the snowbank without molestation. He jumped out and we hauled Mrs. Logan's casket out and pushed it into the bed of the pickup. It was kind of awkward with two people transferring a casket but she didn't weigh much and we were able to do it. The driver had his cigarette clamped between his teeth with an ash so long I have no idea how it didn't fall off with all the jostling and grunting we did to get Mrs. Logan into his truck. But we did, and the ash remained. "Cord in the back," the man said and climbed back into the cab of his truck.

I bungeed the casket into the truck bed and opened the passenger door. The driver swept a mound of McDonald's Styrofoam containers, empty cigarette packs and loose shotgun shells into the foot well. "Hop in," he said. "Where we goin'?"

"Northlake."

He gave me a blank look.

"I'll guide you." I stuck out my hand. "By the way, I'm Casey. Casey Poe."

He wiped his hand on his mountain man beard and took mine. "Chip."

"Pleased to meet you."

He grunted and the long ash fell into his lap. "Wherewegoin'?"

"Okay, turn around and head back the way you were coming from," I said.

He gunned the engine and the truck bucked out of the snow and onto the road. He took a long pull on his cigarette and eyed me out the corner of his watery eye. "By the way, man, what the fuck happened to your nose?"

We pulled into Northlake Memorial Park forty-five minutes late. I think it's a facet of the profession; every funeral director I know is fanatical about time. I'd rather be half an hour early than one minute late. So I was climbing the pickup truck walls with anxiety as Chip peppered me with questions about boxing. I was so anxious about facing the Logan family, I didn't even want to go in and face them. *What am I going to tell these people? How am I going to explain the truck... How am I going to explain Chip?* These thoughts swirled through my head as Chip pulled up in front of the office. Thankfully, my feet automatically jumped out and took me to the office, because the rest of me was rebelling.

The Logan family was sitting in the tiny office. Kerry jumped up and said, "Casey! Thank God you made it. We called your office and they said you had left two and a half hours ago. We thought something had happened to you!"

I smiled a little. I felt like I was going to puke. Instead, I said, "Sorry I'm late. I got a little stuck."

A very tan man in a finely cut suit that I assumed to be

Kerry's brother got up and confirmed it. "Tom Logan," he said, offering his hand.

I shook it.

"Oh, no! You did?" Kerry said from behind her brother.

"Glad you got unstuck," Tom said smoothly. He smelled of cologne and expensive moisturizer.

"I didn't," I said.

"You didn't?" Tom echoed.

"How'd you get here?" Kerry asked.

"I hitched a ride."

Kerry and Tom cocked their heads in unison.

"And Mom?" Kerry asked slowly.

Instead of explaining I waved a soggy glove at them. "Come on, I'll show you."

They crowded out onto the office steps of Northlake Memorial Park to see the dented, jacked up pickup truck idling roughly with a casket in the back, and Chip, seeing as he was center stage, waved a hand out the window and yelled, "Howdy folks!" He was going for the world record with his newest cigarette ash.

"A plow ran me off the road in the nature preserve and I waited for over an hour before Chip here came along. It would've been nightfall before I found someone to winch the hearse out, and I knew how important it was to you that we do the burial today with all the family present."

I braced myself for the tempest that was surely to come. At the very least, I expected a comment from Tom, but instead he held up his hand and said gravely, "We understand, and thank you, Casey"—he placed his arm around my shoulders—"for making this day happen for us. The mode of transportation isn't important, just the fact that you got mother here so we could bury her."

I released the giant breath I had been holding. I felt like I

wanted to puke, but the winning kind; the feeling you get
after a fight when you've gone the distance and are just so
relieved you want to...puke. I had gone the distance on this
one and taken some licks, but in the end the ref had held my
hand up.

I said as lightly as I could, "So, shall we go over to the
grave?"

"Sounds good," Tom said and clapped me on the back.
"You lead the way."

"Hey, mister," one of the little boys, probably a grandson
of Kerry's, piped up. He was wearing a little black suit with a
topcoat over it and wingtips. He looked like a mini-
undertaker.

"Yeah?"

"What happened to your nose?"

Three Requiems for Two Caskets
Contributed by an angler

There wasn't a cloud in the sky. It was a picturesque
sunny day in the Big Easy—the perfect day for a jazz funeral.

The morning was just transitioning to afternoon, and thus
the streets hadn't swelled with the revelers that would come
later in the evening, though one could smell the stale smells
wafting from the gin mills and jazz clubs. The flies hung fat
and lazy in the thick humidity, their buzzing the only sound
as the musicians quietly assembled in small throngs.

When the funeral service ended, the doors to the church
flew open, and the crowd spilled onto the streets. Mrs.
Drouillard's casket, gleaming in the early afternoon light, was
borne down the steps on the shoulders of pallbearers in a
menagerie of costumes ranging from formal to casual, but all
wearing the white cotton gloves denoting their chosen role.

The band sprang into action with the arrival of the guest

of honor. They sputtered to life almost in stages, out of tune for a couple of measures, before finding their groove and launching into a raucous tune more fitting for a Mardis Gras parade than a funeral anthem. Their musical ecstasy wasn't a product of the occasion as much it was as their time spent prior to assembling on the church steps at the corner watering hole drinking Sazerac and beer and passing around hip flasks of rye on the church steps as they grew weary of waiting for Reverend Wright to wrap it up.

A sea of the white-shirted musicians, guests brandishing umbrellas to ward off the intense sun rays, and, of course, the bobbing casket, made its way down the road to the cemetery where mausolea lined the drives like rows and rows of tiny white residential homes. Random whistle calls punctuated the air like figurative exclamation points. As the musicians got closer to the cemetery their fervor picked up. It might have been due to the alcohol, or the excited tourists, busy snapping photos, hooting and hollering, and joining the seemingly impromptu parade, that fueled their revelry.

The scene was vintage Creole, quintessential New Orleans.

When the band got to the site of the mausoleum they crescendoed and then suddenly fell silent like someone flicking a light switch off.

As the band exited the cemetery gates, their song was a subdued, somber dirge that almost sounded like a song of defeat. One might think it to, in fact, be just that since the casket followed in tow.

In a court of law I'd be accused of hearsay. I didn't actually see the event. Felix Maistre recounted it to me, and I conjured up the rest in my imagination. But I do know the back story; I know why the band's sails lost their wind. I was a part of that back-story that led up to the band *leaving* the cemetery with the casket.

My father has this idiom, "quality pays; it doesn't cost," and though it's just an expression, I think it's very salient advice. It can be applied to any aspect of life where an economic choice can be made: cars, clothes, laundry detergent, televisions, et cetera. You name it, you have a monetary "vote" you can make...even when purchasing caskets. But vote wisely because, as long as we're being axiomatic, some people are pennywise and pound foolish.

Used to be if you wanted a casket you bought it from the man that peddled funeral wares: the town's undertaker. Nowadays you can go to the big-box stores and at the end of aisle 20—the aisle with the three-hundred-count toilet paper rolls and gross box of five million AA batteries—are the caskets. I picture some guy yelling to his wife as he goes out the door, "Hey Marlene, I'm going down to the [insert store name of choice] and get a twenty-pack of shaving cream, a skid of fruit pies, and our caskets. You need anything?"

And if you don't happen to live near one of those soul-sucking stores there's this new thing called the Internet where caskets can be purchased for cheap, real cheap! "Why pay the inflated retail prices of a funeral home? Get any casket shipped to the funeral parlor's door within two days," or some such claim one of these hundreds of Internet casket retail websites brags.

I hope I don't come off like some old dog growling over a bone. I certainly advocate consumer rights and choices. Hey, I like a good deal as much as the next guy, but: buyer beware. It's not like ordering a book off the Internet versus buying it in the store. Not all caskets are created equal. And federal law mandates that we, the funeral directors, don't require consumers to purchase a casket from us. So, if you order something from a big box store or off the Internet we *have* to accept it. It's the law. And that's where Buckey and Brenda and the big brass band come in.

I pegged them for transplants the minute they walked through the door. I think their loud Hawaiian shirts gave them away.

"Hello, I'm Roger," I said and stepped forward to the couple, hand extended.

The rest of the introductions were made, and my suspicions were confirmed. Their bayou accent was strong. I ushered them into my office. After we all sat down, and I offered them coffee, I issued them our GPL, a document the FTC requires funeral parlors to provide. The GPL, or general price list, is kind of like a menu; it lists *everything* the funeral parlor offers, even the kitchen sink. Right away Buckey set the tone by getting out a pen and small calculator from a breast pocket, which was overflowing with pens and papers, and began going through the GPL crossing stuff off, muttering to himself, "No, we won't need that, no, no, no—"

"Sir," I said, "once we talk a little bit about funeral arrangements I will be able to point you to which items on the GPL will pertain to your situation."

Buckey paused and peered at me over his half glasses. "I know what we need," he said before returning to his calculations.

"Okay," I said briskly, and let him go about his scribblings and calculations while I gathered biographical information from Brenda about her mother. We drafted a death notice, and scheduled funeral plans. We were going to be holding a funeral service in our parlor and then shipping Mrs. Drouillard back to New Orleans (or as they called it, N'Awlins) for another funeral service and burial in her family plot.

"Now," I said, clicking my pen and passing both of them copies of our casket price list, "the matter of the casket."

I hardly had time to get the sentence out of my mouth when Buckey cut in. "Already been taken care of."

"Excuse me?" I asked, caught a little off balance.

Buckey sat back in his chair and tore off his half-moon glasses and tossed them on the desk. "I have already purchased the casket," he said.

"Oh?"

"I bought it online." He smiled like he had just pulled one over on me. Buckey snatched his glasses and the casket price list off the desktop and after perching the glasses at the tip of his nose, flipped through the price list. "Yeah," he said to no one in particular, "I'm not paying these exorbitant prices." The glasses landed back on the desk.

I was a little put off by his tone, but didn't let it show. "That's perfectly your right," I said. "I'll just ask that you make yourself available to come to the funeral parlor when the casket arrives. That way you can inspect it for any damage before I take delivery of it. Or, if you can't make yourself available, I have a damage waiver for you to sign."

He looked at me with a puckered face for a moment, as if trying to decide if I was punishing him for buying a casket online; deciding I wasn't, and that he had won, he broke into a huge grin, and said, "Done! Just tell me when and where."

Before Buckey and Brenda left, I called Felix Maistre, the mortician in N'Awlins who would be servicing the other end of the funeral to give him the details.

"Ms. Drouillard? Sure, I know her family well," he said in his long drawl. "My daddy and granddaddy buried most all of her kin."

I imagined Felix in some dark mortuary under massive cypress trees dutifully copying down all the information. When I was finished, he said, "Now, Rodg-uh (Roger), I assume since you're having a service there in Arizona she'll be coming furnished."

That's industry talk that means the body is being shipped somewhere in a casket. I confirmed that she was, in fact, coming furnished.

"You have to be careful when ordering the casket to make sure it fits. The crypt opening is small by today's standards. You only have about a twenty-eight-inch crypt-width if memory serves me correctly. Make sure you provide them with a casket that will fit that width."

N'Awlins is below sea level. Basically, if you drive a shovel into the soil you have hit water. Therefore all of their cemeteries have aboveground crypts and mausolea, and not in-ground burials like most people are used to seeing. For clarification purposes, a mausoleum is a building that has several crypts, or "slots," within it depending on the size of the mausoleum, while an aboveground crypt (depending whether it is single or double) is almost like a box sitting on the ground for one or two caskets. In N'Awlins they put the body in the crypt until another family member needs it. At which point they then rake the bones out, put them in an ossuary, or special place for bones, which is oftentimes in the crypt itself, destroy the casket, and re-use the crypt. A family can use the same crypt space for generations.

"Hold on," I said and held my hand over the mouthpiece. "Felix says the crypt opening is only twenty-eight inches, at best, which is really narrow. Most crypts today have an opening of around thirty to thirty-two inches to accommodate almost all modern caskets. Do you have the outside dimensions on this casket you ordered?"

Buckey waved his hand at me. "It'll fit."

He didn't seem positive.

"Are you sure?" I asked.

"Oh, yeah. It'll fit."

"Okay," I said dubiously and uncovered the mouthpiece.

"The family has purchased the casket from an outside vendor and has told me it will fit."

"Outside vendor?" Felix seemed puzzled by the notion.

"Off the Internet," I clarified.

"We don't get much of that down here in N'Awlins. But okay, just make sure they are aware of the crypt width."

"They're aware," I said.

We bade good-bye and I went over the funeral bill with the couple.

Two days later, I was rousted away from the dinner table with my wife and three kids to go to the funeral parlor and meet some guy named Ned driving a beat-up panel van delivering Buckey's casket. Buckey showed up wearing an even louder Hawaiian shirt, a feat I had previously thought impossible, and went over the casket with a fine-tooth comb before deeming it worthy of delivery. "Wait," I said before the deliveryman could unload, and ran into the funeral parlor for a tape measure. I measured the top and bottom molding of the casket. Twenty-eight inches exactly. "You sure you want this?" I asked Buckey. "The bottom molding is exactly the crypt opening. It may not fit."

"Funeral is day after tomorrow," he said. "It took three days for this to get here. I'm stuck with it."

"I can get you something I know will fit in time," I said.

"What? And pay your prices?" he scoffed. "Believe me, I'll make it fit. It just might have to go in on an angle."

"Even a sixteenth of an inch variation is going to make it very hard, maybe impossible, to get it in," I cautioned.

"If worst comes to worst, we'll just put it in sideways."

"Okay. Unload her," I told Ned.

The day after the next we had the funeral and I drove Mrs. Drouillard to the airport. Two days after I waved goodbye to Mrs. Drouillard, I received a call from Felix Maistre.

"Mr. Perry," he said, "we had a little problem with the casket you sent."

"Oh?" I said.

"It didn't fit."

"Really?" I said, playing dumb. "I gave the family the crypt measurements you provided me, and they assured me it would."

He began to recount, in vivid detail, Mrs. Drouillard's funeral. I felt like I was being read a graphic novel and having the pictures described to me. When Felix got to the part where the entire funeral party was crypt-side he said, "We tried every which way to push that casket in there but it simply wouldn't fit."

"What did you do?"

"The musicians just died," Felix said. I didn't think he intended it to be a witticism. "They had peaked when we reached the crypt-side; they had nothing left, pallbearers too. But what else could I do? I had the pallbearers carry her back to the mortuary with the band leading the way. Oh, you should have heard them leaving the cemetery; it was most somber band I've ever heard."

"I bet. Has Mrs. Drouillard been laid to rest?" I asked.

"Oh yes," he said. "I re-casketed Ms. Drouillard at the mortuary in a casket that would fit into the crypt, and back to the cemetery we went. And let me tell you something, the third time around the band was even worse! It isn't a far distance from the mortuary to the cemetery but it was a *long* walk. You'd think by the way the band played the third time that someone had died."

CHAPTER 11

The People

W hat about the people who work in a mortuary? They've got to be a bunch of Lurch-like characters who have some unnatural obsession with death, right? Not really. The cast of *The Office* is much stranger than anyone I have encountered during my career. Granted, the nature of the job calls for us to be polite, friendly—though not overly so— and slightly detached. The casual guest at a wake might find us slightly aloof, though in reality we aren't.

In this first story we look at some superstitions some funeral directors have with death. Zippy is a sedatephobic, and explains how he got so in this story along with his two compatriots who also have interesting superstitions. Dave counts flowers and Jen can't stop crossing herself.

But what exactly is a superstition and where do they come from? Webster's defines it as "an irrational belief in or notion of the ominous significance of a particular thing, circumstance, occurrence, et cetera; a custom or act based on such a belief." Some of these superstitions are religiously rooted, and others, I imagine, evolve organically like Zippy's. Later in the book, you'll notice an example of a folklore-oriented superstition with Bob in "After [Death]." Personally, I haven't developed any superstitions and don't work with anyone with any noticeable superstitions, though it may be more prevalent in this profession than others because we deal with the big unknown: death.

Superstitions aside, I think you'll find us a pretty down-to-earth group. Most of us do the job because we enjoy being around people, and I have yet to find a funeral director who isn't personable. So, along that personality vein, we included a story about a dewy-eyed funeral director (with marriage aspirations of her own) playing matchmaker and creating a very unlikely friendship.

Even Flowers, Odd People
Contributed by a traveler

You know what a funeral director with a broken leg can do? Pretty much nothing. I couldn't go on removals, I couldn't embalm, I couldn't go on errands because, of course, I broke my right leg and therefore couldn't drive, and I couldn't go on funerals because I couldn't roll a casket up an aisle. I became the Quasimodo of the funeral home, relegated to making funeral arrangements and performing secretarial work. It wasn't very glamorous, but I did find I was still able to get out from behind a desk and move flowers around.

The doctor gave me a scooter.

It was one of those leg scooters for gimpy people. It has four wheels, handlebars with a hand brake, and a cushion to put under your knee. I had broken my tibia and a couple of ankle bones, so the cast was only from the knee down and encased my foot. On these scooters you use your good leg to propel yourself around—like Fred Flintstone. It's kind of like one of those walkers with a seat, but not really.

I found I could get some serious speed in the back hall of the funeral home where it's a straight, tiled run; hence the new name that was bestowed upon me by Pat, one of the ladies in the office: Zippy.

I squinted at the tag on the flower basket. It read: *Funeral Services of Mrs. Lena Green.* One-handed, so as not to lose my balance, I hefted the basket onto my shoulder like a waiter shouldering a big tray. I glanced at my watch and rolled out of the flower delivery room. I pumped my good leg and gathered speed in the back hall until I was doing a good clip, nearly taking out Pat as she exited the ladies room, turned the corner into the lobby on two wheels, threaded the parlor doors, and applied pressure to the handbrake, coming to an abrupt stop at the casket.

"There," I said, puffing from exertion, slinging the papier-mâché basket off my shoulder, "that's the last of them." I looked at my watch. Fifty-seven seconds. It was a new speed record. I was thrilled.

"Okay," Dave said, stepping back from the casket.

I could tell by his tone he wasn't listening to me. He was too busy counting flowers.

His lips moved silently and his finger danced over a standing spray of flowers. Shaking his head, he stepped up to the spray and removed a flower, and then stepped back. He counted again, and satisfied, nodded, and looked at me as if surprised and asked, "Jesus, Zip, why are you breathing so heavy?"

"New speed record."

He looked at me like I was nuts.

I shrugged. I was so bored helping Pat with paperwork, this is what I had resorted to: setting speed records in my scooter.

"That the last of them?"

I nodded; I knew he had been too preoccupied with the flowers to hear my earlier statement. But that's what Dave does, he counts flowers. If he comes up with an odd number he pulls a flower out. There *has* to be an even number in each flower arrangement.

Dave's mother is Eastern European, Hungarian, I think, and in their culture it's bad luck to have an odd number of flowers in a funeral arrangement. Dave takes it to the extreme. He can't rest until he is *positive* each and every floral piece has an even number. I'm not too sure what he thinks will happen; the person is already dead. For a larger funeral, with many floral pieces, Dave will be in the viewing parlor counting flowers for hours. I'm not sure if Dave's infatuation with flowers can be classified as a superstition or OCD. Whatever it is, it's debilitating.

"Okay then," I said, "if you're good up here Pat has some veteran's forms for me to fill out." Pat was starting to treat me like her assistant. I hoped she wasn't getting too used to it because as soon as I could walk she was returning to her job as *my* assistant.

"Uh-huh, Zip," Dave said absentmindedly as he stepped back to do a recount.

I executed a squeaky three-point turn on the hardwood floor with my scooter, churned down the aisle between the parlor chairs, rethreaded the parlor doors, and gathered speed down the hallway.

By the time I got to my office door I had to be doing three hundred miles per hour; I jammed on the brakes, and was about to execute a gem of a J-turn just when Jen stepped out of my office door.

She jumped aside to avoid getting mowed down and screamed. "Damnit, Zip!" She put her hand over her heart and took a deep breath. "Stop driving that thing around like a maniac," she scolded.

I grinned. "Sorry. I have to find some way of entertaining myself. What do you need?"

"You working the viewing this evening?"

"Dave."

"Great." She pantomimed his lips moving and the finger counting. His obsession with even flowers drove her crazy.

I laughed at her impression and rolled into my office and she, presumably, went to find Dave. I still haven't figured out why she makes fun of Dave. She's just as superstitious as he is.

Jen crosses herself every time she comes across a dead body. *Spectacles, testicles, watch, and wallet,* is my silent mantra every time I see her standing over one of the dearly departed doing her furtive hand motions. Needless to say, working as the greeter in a funeral home, Jen crosses herself an awful lot during the course of a day.

Of course, since I'm casting stones I can't leave myself out. I'll tell you about my recent idiosyncrasy, though I don't think it's a superstition, per se. It's more of an . . . oddity. I whistle.

I didn't always whistle, but now I do it to cut the silence.

A funeral home is a mighty still place at night. Mighty still. The families that live in them will tell you, "Yeah, it's a nice quiet place to live." What they don't tell you is that funeral homes are so quiet that you can hear your heart beating—almost like an alternate version of "The Tell-Tale Heart." It's that type of pervasive, suffocating silence.

When I'm alone in the viewing parlors, I whistle or sing just so there is some sort of noise. It's not a problem in the prep room because I have a little radio and at my desk I can stream music or talk shows from the web. But in the rest of the funeral home I have to do something so I'm not overwhelmed by the claustrophobic silence.

The silence didn't used to bother me. In fact, it was kind of nice compared to my previous jobs when I was a kid working at a carnival where the lights and bells and buzzers never ceased, and at a lunch counter with the phone ringing incessantly and people screaming orders for Italian hoagies and ham and Swiss on rye with spicy mustard across the counter. Yes, the silence was *very* nice at first.

But then the other shoe dropped.

And now I can't stand the silence *and* it earned me a broken leg.

It was April. We weren't having the normal "April showers" type rains, more like a deluge of biblical proportions for the entire month. We were having construction done on the funeral home, and the rain was delaying progress. The construction crew couldn't pour footers because the holes were like miniature swimming pools. They'd get a day's respite and the bilge pumps would be fired up only to be overwhelmed the following day. Of course it was entrance construction that kept getting delayed which meant for those deconstruct/reconstructing months we were forced to run all funeral traffic through the backdoor.

On a particular night of that rainy month when the footers weren't being poured I had a viewing, so, after applying makeup to Mrs. Longbow, reciting the mantra silently while Jen crossed herself over the body, arranging the flowers around the casket, having Dave count them, and filling out the guest book, I left to eat dinner before the calling hours. For those of you who aren't familiar with the jargon, that's what we refer to as the time during the viewing, because it is the time you can call on the family and pay your respects.

I arrived back at the funeral home about an hour before the calling hours were to begin. It was raining, as it had been doing all month. During my mad dash into the funeral home to try to keep my suit somewhat dry, I noticed Pat's car was in the parking lot. I expected to find her busy at her desk catching up on paperwork, but as I shook giant droplets from my navy pinstripe I couldn't find her in the office or the kitchenette.

I was all alone in the funeral home.

I wasn't too puzzled. Sometimes her husband swung by the funeral home on his way home from work and picked her up and they went out to eat.

This must be one of those nights, I mused.

Knowing the Longbow family was due to arrive in a half hour, I busied myself brewing coffee and arranging a box of fresh-baked, assorted cookies from a local bakery onto a silver serving platter. I emptied the trash cans in the restrooms and made sure they were stocked up on toilet paper, hand towels, and soap, gave the lobby a quick once-over with the vacuum, and filled the coffee urns and set out the baked goods on the coffee service bar. Surveying my work, I decided the lobby was ready to receive visitors. The only thing I had left to do was to double-check the makeup on Mrs. Longbow and set out a pitcher of water for the family to use in case they got parched from talking to all their guests.

I went to the kitchenette and retrieved a pitcher from the refrigerator.

The parlor was quiet and still as a tomb when I entered— the lighting dim like a Hollywood movie might depict a tomb. We keep it dim for a reason; it makes the reposed look better. But there are a lot of shadowy corners due to the low lighting and rich draperies that gobble the remaining photons up.

The air conditioner had overcooled the room, purposely. Two hundred people give off a lot of body heat. I had kicked the air back to combat the ensuing visitors. I couldn't hear it running, but I could smell its thin, metallic scent as its tendrils floated from the overhead diffusers.

Thu-thump, thu-thump went my heart in chilly and thick silence.

It was just the dead and me.

All alone.

Without warning, the quiet was shattered by a LOUD voice. "Hi, Bill."

The blood froze right in my veins. Literally froze solid in my veins.

I'm alone, right?

The cut crystal pitcher, forgotten, dropped right out my hand and shattered.

The fight-or-flight urge was overwhelming me to *flee, flee!* I reeled around to see where the noise was coming from. In my haste, I slipped on the slick surface caused by the broken pitcher on the glossy hardwoods.

I did a brief jerking, ungraceful dance like I was a marionette, my feet becoming entangled in a chair. I knew I was going down. And I did, my leg levering between the chair legs.

When I hit the ground, I felt something pop and then a stinging pain. It felt like somebody had punched me in the gut; the wind was knocked out of me.

Then I saw him.

"Mr. Longbow," I croaked, from my position on the floor.

There he sat, sitting stock still, pressed out in his funereal finest, in a chair next to the head of the casket, hidden in the gloomy ebb of a shadow created by the special lighting used to illuminate his wife. He shifted forward, the light splashing on his face. "Oh, my," he said, "Did I startle you?"

No, I always scream like a girl and fall to the floor. The pain had started as a dull ache and quickly blossomed.

He cocked his head. "Bill, are you all right?"

I tried to move. A wave of pain made me cry out involuntarily.

He got up and came over to move the chair. I waved him away frantically. I didn't want him disturbing my leg. "Call an ambulance," I managed to croak out.

I was all night in the emergency room and for my troubles got a cast on my leg all the way down to the ankle. My tibia had broken cleanly, and a couple of ankle bones for good measure. And I got stitches in two different places, for a total of seventeen stitches, after they extracted a couple shards of crystal from my leg.

I took a day off to convalesce and sleep and the following day I wheeled into the business office on my new scooter. I was quite the sight: suit pant leg cut up the side to accommodate the cast.

"Jesus, Bill! What happened to you?" Pat asked.

I didn't answer her question, but asked one of my own. "Did you leave your car at the funeral home the other evening for some reason?"

"No."

"You sure you and Joe didn't go out to dinner the night before last?"

"No," she replied in a tone that suggested I might be stupid. "Why?"

Mr. Longbow must have the same car, I thought. "Did you forget to do something at the funeral home when you left?"

"Like..." She really drew the word out.

"Forget to lock the backdoor," I finished for her.

There was silence as she mentally retraced her steps before she simply said, "Oh. Sorry." Then there was another pause. "Why?"

"Well," I said, "the husband of the deceased decided to arrive extra, extra early while I was home eating dinner. And, upon finding the building unlocked just came on in and sat in the parlor with his wife. I arrived and saw what I *thought* was your car in the lot. When you weren't inside, I figured you had gone out to eat with Joe. So I tidied up for a half hour before taking a pitcher of water into the parlor." I paused for dramatic effect. "Mr. Longbow was sitting quietly in a chair and I didn't notice him until he called out"—I raised my voice two octaves and shouted—"Hey Bill!" In a real quiet tone I said, "That's when *I* did the dance with the chair." I motioned with my head down toward the scooter. "And snapped my leg."

Once she paused her laughter, I resumed in a normal tone, "I thought I was alone in the building. So you see, it's a good thing I have a strong heart, or else it may not have been an ambulance that came to pick me up. It could've been the medical examiner."

"Don't be so dramatic," she said.

"Are you kidding me? I've been having nightmares about this."

"What are you afraid of? The dead coming to get you?"

Ms. Sympathy, I thought. "Well, I didn't used to!"

"Please," she scoffed. "Look, if it'll make you feel better, I'll even sign your cast."

"Forget the cast," I said. "Look at the sweet ride they issued me. I can pop a wheelie in this thing." I landed the front wheels on her desk.

I received a lovely card from Mr. Longbow wishing me a speedy recovery. I thought it ironic, the bereaved sending the funeral director the card, but it was a very nice gesture on his part. After seven weeks the cast came off, the beloved scooter went by the wayside, but the name Zippy stuck, as did the sedatephobia—fear of silence. Though it's not really the quiet that bothers me; it's the prospect of having that silence shattered unexpectedly that sends a shiver down my back. It bothers me so much so that I now find myself leaving the television on at night in my own house.

The profession seems to attract them, the superstitious. I'm not sure what the reasoning behind that is, but perhaps it's the fact that the profession is so married to religion, and a lot of our little rituals centered on the dead are based religiously. You find superstitions in everyday life, but rarely in the workplace. I've never heard of an accountant eating a certain breakfast in the morning to bring him luck preparing taxes for the coming day, or a physician snapping his fingers three times after administering an injection so it'll "take." That's preposterous. But then again, those professions are based in science, while mine is one involving one of the greatest unknowns. Death. So I guess a little superstition to help the dead along to the place they need to get isn't such a bad thing.

I've convinced Dave that he must've miscounted Mrs. Longbow's flowers and let an odd number slip by. He has since apologized.

Two Funerals and a Wedding
Contributed by an amateur pâtissière

My fiancé asked me for the umpteenth time as he snugged his tie in front of the mirror, "Why are we being invited, again?"

"Because I introduced the bride and groom," I replied, trying not to let the exasperation I was feeling creep into my voice as I applied the finishing touches to my makeup.

Sam turned from the mirror to show me. He looked like a
stuffed sausage in his suit and I don't think even a sailor
could decipher his necktie knot. Sam's not a tie-type guy; he
probably wears one twice a year. Unlike the guys I work with
who wear a coat and tie to go to the gym, Sam would rather
catch the bubonic plague than wear a tie.

I went over and started to work on his tie knot. "This is
pathetic."

"I don't ever need to wear one of these damn things!"

"I thought you had to learn at least how to tie one, not
necessarily wear one, before you could get your guy card," I
said, tugging and pulling.

"Shut up. You tie these things all day long." He decided to
start back on the event. "Don't you even think it's a little
strange that they invited the town undertaker to their
wedding. I mean, it's not like you're a friend who also
happens to be the town undertaker."

"Hold still," I grunted. I pulled, cinched, and smoothed,
noting with satisfaction it was a perfect Windsor knot.
"There, all done," I cooed in a mothering tone. "You can just
stop your bellyaching. I think it's nice they invited us.
Besides, there'll be an open bar, and I'm sure you'll make
plenty of friends hanging out there."

I could tell he had been adequately soothed by the
prospect of free booze, but he insisted on getting the last
comment in. "I'm just saying," he grumbled, "it seems a little
strange."

Yes, it is an unusual invitation, I thought. But we had
been invited, and we were going. And go we did and Sam
had a good time in spite of himself. And despite his
protestations I was not the Angel of Death at a wedding. We
blended in with all the other dewy-eyed twenty- or thirty-
somethings reveling in the magic of marriage, which was

especially poignant in view of the ages of the bride and bridegroom.

It was a particularly busy week when the soon-to-be newlyweds met. So busy, in fact, we were hosting two or three visitations a night. In the lobby on the night Marianne and Greg crossed paths, we had two of those signs out that have the felt grooves that you push the little white plastic letters into. One sign in front of the chapel said WESLEY VISITATION, 5–8 P.M. The one in front of the memorial hall said INGRAM VISITATION, 5–8 P.M.

I find those signs useful to a varying degree. Most people blow into the lobby, ignore me and the signs, and just head into *a* room and then come out bitching. "Is this the John Doe visitation? I'm in the wrong place!" And I feel like saying to them, "Ma'am or Sir, if you have taken time to pause and listen to my greeting *or* read these handy dandy signs you practically tripped over, you'd have known which way to go."

But I hold my tongue and pleasantly say, "Right this way," and smile. I realize mortuaries put people on edge, and I try not to be too judgmental.

It was shortly after five p.m. when Mrs. Wesley emerged from the chapel. The best I can describe her is "grand-motherly." She reminded me a lot of my late grandmother, very regal looking, but with a real sweet demeanor. "Lisa," she whispered to me, "would it be possible to turn the music down a bit?" She said it as if it were the biggest imposition she had ever asked anyone, and it pained her to do so.

"Not a problem," I replied.

"Everything is just great," she said and placed a hand on my forearm. She smelled like grandmother perfume and cinnamon gum. "Everyone has been commenting on how great Bobby looks. He looks ten years younger."

I smiled and nodded. "Glad you're pleased with everything. Now you better get back into your guests. I'll turn the music down."

She held up her index and thumb together. "Just a smidge."

"Okay." As I turned to comply with her request, a man caught Mrs. Wesley's eye.

"Greg? Greg Ingram?" she called.

The man, familiar to me, turned.

"So good of you to come!" Mrs. Wesley said and hurried over to him.

The man stood in the lobby like a deer in headlights. He obviously didn't recognize this woman.

She embraced him and then held him at arm's length. "You're looking great!"

"Uh, thanks," he replied, unsure of what else to say.

"I can't believe you saw me in the paper, and after all this time thought to come. You always were so sweet like that. What's it been," she gushed, "Fifty years? I think the last time I saw you was that night at Styer's Soda Counter—the night we broke up."

A wave of recognition washed over Mr. Ingram. "Marianne?" He chuckled, like he couldn't believe it, and repeated, "Marianne?"

She looked momentarily confused. "Yes, it's me, Marianne Wesley..." She laughed. "Well, Marianne Ring. Who did you think you were coming to see?"

"Oh my gosh!" Mr. Ingram said. "This is amazing!" A smile broke out on his face, the first one I'd seen grace his countenance in our dealings. "I'm here because the visitation tonight is for my wife, Anita."

"Oh," Marianne said, face turning sympathetic. "I am so sorry."

"Me too," Mr. Ingram said, "for your husband."

Mrs. Wesley reached for his forearm. She seemed to like to do that, hold on to people's forearms while she spoke to them. "It was for the best. Bobby was in a lot of pain for a long time. I'm glad he's with the Lord now."

Mr. Ingram swallowed hard and looked at the ground. "Anita's was rather sudden. The family and I were a little shocked." He chuckled nervously, "Not that at our age any of this"—he motioned around the mortuary with a nod of his head—"should be a shock. I find myself seeing all my friends at funerals. That's the only time I catch up. Must be a sign of our age."

Mrs. Wesley beamed. "I see you still have the same sense of humor."

He smiled in spite of himself. "I didn't think I'd smile at all today, but you brought it out. Tell you what, since you thought I was here for your visitation, I'll sign your guest registry."

They both laughed merrily—a much-needed catharsis—and chatted for another moment before deciding it was time to get back to their guests, at which time they both agreed it had been good seeing one another after so much time.

At the end of the visitation time, both families were leaving at the same time and the paternal and maternal heads introduced their respective families to each other. The next day we conducted the two services and I thought the next time I would see those families would be when I was called upon to service another death in the family. I was wrong.

It had been months and months since the service and I had to rack my brain to recall the service when the receptionist called me on the intercom to tell me I had a call from a Mrs. Wesley. I figured her call had something to do with a detail relating to the funeral. Perhaps she needed more death certificates.

"Lisa," she started, "Greg and I would like to invite you to our wedding."

I was caught off guard. "Me?" I asked idiotically. I had no idea who Greg was and why a widow was inviting me to her wedding.

She laughed in her airy way. "Yes. Greg and I feel that since you played a role in reintroducing us that you should partake in our day, that is if you aren't working."

When she said that it all came flooding back to me. "Yeah, yeah, that would be wonderful," I said, recovering. I noted Mrs. Wesley had been gracious enough to give me an out if I wanted to refuse the invitation.

"I know it's all so sudden, but you can't fight fate, you know?" she said. "So you'll come?"

"I'd be honored to attend," I said.

"Wonderful! I wanted to call and ask first so you didn't get a strange invitation to a wedding in the mail."

"No, no, it's perfectly all right. Thank you."

Mrs. Wesley went on to explain how she and Greg had started having coffee together and reconnecting and helping each other through their grief. Their coffee dates turned into lunch and then dinners, until they just decided to get married. "At our age, there's no sense waiting. We make each other happy. And I know it's only been nine months since the funerals, but no sense playing coy with each other like we're silly teenagers again. Our families are behind the marriage one hundred percent."

I thought about how I had waited for five years to get a ring from Sam, and then had to do the undelicate and unladylike job of picking out my own ring and asking him to marry me. The poor boy has many, many good qualities, but in that category he is clueless. "Yup," I agreed, "no sense being coy."

Mrs. Wesley, even though in her seventies, outlined the details of the wedding to me like some giddy bride a half century her junior. I listened with rapt attention. I think women of any age just eat weddings up. Me included. Just issue me a spoon.

It was going to be a fairly small ceremony in her son's backyard, but they were renting chairs and building a white altar with pillars and white lace bunting. It was going to be catered: butlered, heavy hors d'oeuvres, and of course an open bar. I told Mrs. Wesley, who insisted on me calling her "Marianne," that everything sounded wonderful. I couldn't wait to attend.

You never know who you're going to run into in life, or who is going to change the course of it. It can happen in the supermarket or at a . . . funeral. You just have to know when that proverbial door has been opened for you, and have the courage to go through it.

Mrs. Wesley and Mr. Ingram shared eight happy years of marriage. I know because we exchanged Christmas cards each year, and theirs always included a handwritten note from Marianne telling me about their previous year. Sadly, after that eighth year I received a call from Marianne. Her husband had died, and could I come over?

I went from being the undertaker being invited to a wedding, to being a friend who also happened to be an undertaker.

There are the people who work at the funeral home, but there are also the people who attend the funerals. We see *all* manner of people and situations at funerals. Though I have been at this less than a decade, at the end of each day I feel like I have seen it all. The next day something surprises me. That's what I love about the job.

In *MC:USTD* we touched on some of that—the everyday: the fistfights, gun fights, prima donnas, princes, thieves, and paupers, and all the rest that Elton John would just lump together and call, "Mona Lisas and Mad Hatters." But we see those people on a daily basis. What about something very different? What about a professional funeral crasher? It sounds like something out of the movies—*Wedding Crashers*, specifically. But Marla is real.

Don't get this confused with a professional mourner. They are paid to come to funerals and wail, and aren't uncommon. Marla is a person who comes to funerals not knowing a soul, with the sole intent of crashing it.

How do you crash a funeral, you ask?

Read on.

All it took was an observant funeral director with a big appetite to figure out there was somebody crashing funerals.

The Funeral Crasher
Contributed by a former track runner

Who *wants* to go to a funeral? Nobody. We try to dress funerals up with twenty-first-century, politically correct, feel-good semantics like "Celebration of Life." But they're not celebrations. Funerals are mournful ceremonies meant to mark the end of a loved one's life. They're sad, depressing occasions that most people try to avoid more than a root canal... that is unless you're a professional funeral crasher. I don't mean a paid mourner; I mean a person who goes to funerals as their job, their means of making a living—a professional funeral crasher (okay, I'm making that title up, but not the "job").

My discovery of Marla, the crasher, all started with the battle of the bulge—my waistline.

These days I try to stay as fit as I can; I have to lift dead weight every day and it takes a strong back. To keep in shape I run several miles each day and lift weights. I manage to keep myself in pretty decent shape (read between the lines: barely passable by my doctor's standards), but there was a time not too long ago, right after I started in the business, when I started developing the dreaded "funeral director's physique" (read between the lines again: I was quite corpulent and my doctor was very upset with me).

I think a funeral director's physique is pretty self-explanatory, but I'll clarify anyway: the body shape is generally classified by a gut, flab, bad skin, and bulbous nose, or any combination of the aforementioned. The body type can be obtained by eating too much or drinking too much, or both.

I started earning my funeral director's physique when I made the mistake of accepting invitations to every reception—sometimes called a repast—following every funeral. That method is generally accepted as the easiest way the funeral director's physique can be achieved in the shortest amount of time. Chocolate cake, pasta salad, mac 'n' cheese, brownies, homemade pies, croissant sandwiches, cocktail meatballs, cold cuts, hoagies, fried chicken, and all that other good comfort food started adding serious inches to my waistline. I didn't notice at first, but after four years of gorging at funeral luncheons, my high school varsity track team body had turned into a junior funeral director's physique—small gut, acne breakouts, and some minor flab.

It was at those luncheons I discovered Marla.

While I was bellied up to the buffet line and stuffing my gob with goodies, I began noticing a reoccurring face. It seemed like no matter which fire hall, church hall, VFW, country club, or restaurant ballroom I went to, I saw the same woman. I couldn't figure out whom she knew, because she seemed to be at so many. Was she a member of a large family? Was she a community leader or local politician? Was she some sort of activist? All those thoughts swirled around in my head. I knew her as a familiar face but I couldn't place her anywhere. It was like she belonged but didn't.

I nicknamed the raven-haired woman Marla because she reminded me of Edward Norton's foil in the movie *Fight Club*. In the movie Marla Singer is the vixen that Ed's character sees at all sorts of support groups, a support group groupie if you will. My Marla seemed to be a funeral groupie.

I was curious, so I started conducting surveillance on her.

And thus, over the next few months, I observed as I gorged.

Marla talked to few people though she might make small talk with someone who she sat near, but she never really *talked* to anyone. Terse mourning smile perpetually plastered on her face, she'd glide in, and like a hummingbird in a field of flowers, flit from one table to another loading her plate with a feast. Then, using her practiced crowd skills, would choose a table that there were a lot of people at, though never any family members. She didn't sit alone, but she obviously sat alone if you know what I mean, her black hair slightly obscuring her face. It was like Marla was white noise, a repast gecko; she simply blended into the background. She was just *there*, and always in the same black mourning attire.

My suspicions grew.

It got to be that I was seeing Marla once a week. Every time I caught her eye or approached her she looked away or fled. Then, there she'd be back next week sitting in the back pew of a church or in the back row of the funeral home or sitting at a crowded table in a noisy church hall.

I was intrigued, so I decided to take the investigation to the next level. I decided to make contact.

I tried chatting her up; it's a skill that's part of the job: being able to make small talk to anyone at the drop of a dime, but it was as if she knew I was pursuing her. Each time I maneuvered so I could talk to her she'd outflank me and retreat.

Finally, one day after many failed attempts, I cornered Marla at the Elk's Lodge.

I spied her sitting somewhat alone at a long table. She was seated against the wall. *Perfect,* I thought. She usually stayed in the relative safety of the pack. *Today the gazelle has fallen behind.* I smiled to myself and lumbered over and tossed down my paper plate loaded with cold cuts and macaroni salad and red velvet cake onto the table next to her. "Hi," I said. My plastic knife and fork, wrapped together in a paper napkin and tied with a piece of red ribbon, sailed down onto the table. I didn't bother to wait for an invitation to sit. I pulled out a chair and sat down next to her, effectively blocking her escape route.

"Hello," she replied. Her face was downcast into her plate of lasagna and salad.

I stuck out my hand. "Name's Dennis."

She shook my hand but didn't offer her name. Her eyes went back down to her plate of food.

"Gee," I said, "you look so familiar." I noisily unwrapped my utensils, struggling with the knot in the bow. "I feel like I've seen you at some funerals before."

"Yeah. I guess. I know a lot of people."

"How do you know the Westins?" I asked, though I pitched it as a friendly inquiry, and not an interrogation question.

"Yeah. I know them." She looked at me quickly, her bright green eyes flashed.

"Really?" I shoveled some macaroni salad into my mouth. "You work with one of the children or something like that?" I asked, my mouth full.

"Uh," she stammered, but recovered quickly and demanded, "Why do you want to know?"

I held up an empty palm. The other claw held a sandwich loaded with cold cuts. "No reason, just making conversation."

"Well, it's none of your business," she shot back defensively. She pushed her plate away and made to get up.

"Look," I said quietly, dropping the act. "Sit down and finish your lunch. I'm not here to give you a hard time. I'm really not. I don't care what you do. I'm just curious... what's your deal?"

She looked at me for a moment with hard eyes, brushing her hair out of her face. Her face suddenly changed, like she had decided she could trust me. Speaking in quick, hushed tones she said, "I live at the shelter." She looked down at the Formica table. "I come to the funerals so I can eat. It's usually the only decent meal I get during the day."

She had confirmed my suspicions that she didn't know any of the families, but I had no idea she was homeless. I felt terrible. "Oh my gosh! I'm sorry. I didn't mean to—"

"No, don't," she said interrupting. "It's okay." She stared at me with an unwavering stare. Her green eyes were intense. "I've been avoiding you because you're the only one who could possibly know. I thought you'd expose me. You're the only one who comes to them all."

I laughed. "I'm the funeral director!"

"No, I mean the luncheons."

Touché.

"Look, I'm not going to expose you. If you go to the funeral, and the family invites everyone that attended the funeral to a luncheon, you're entitled. They invited you. You earned it by attending the service for their loved one." I chewed on the sandwich for a moment, finished it, washed it down with some macaroni salad and picked up another sandwich and bit into it. Still chewing, I asked, "What I want to know is: how do you choose?"

She smiled fleetingly. "I just look for the long obituaries in the paper. I figure it'll be a big crowd at the funeral and I'll be able to remain anonymous at the reception. Sometimes I strike out, but it's been working well for me so far. It's kind of like a job scouting good funerals. I'm something of a professional funeral-goer. I do it all over the city every single day, making sure I don't use the same funeral parlor twice in one week. The ones with several locations, I'll rotate the locations so I maximize the time before I have to go back to a specific location. People like you begin to recognize me."

I nodded. It was clever.

She paused and finished lamely with, "It keeps me well fed."

Finished eating, I stood up and looked at Marla and smiled. "Well good luck to you in your . . . daily searches. Your secret is safe with me."

Those green eyes flashed something that I took to be gratitude.

That day the scale tipped two hundred and twenty and I decided it was time to rid myself of my funeral director's body. I still see Marla at services, about twice a month, but I have stopped attending the repast luncheons to maintain my now (relatively) trim figure.

CHAPTER 12

The Furniture

There's that grand old expression, "never judge a book by its cover," that funeral directors far and wide who are wise abide by when a customer comes calling. The shabbily dressed bag woman with a meek disposition may be a frugal millionaire and buy a bronze casket and pay in cold, hard cash. On the other hand, the flashy looking gentleman who pulls up in a BMW wearing a thousand-dollar suit and a TAG Heuer watch might talk a big game, but may also be up to his eyeballs in debt and stiff you for the funeral bill. It is very tempting to prejudge someone based on their "cover." We all do it, everyday, but it is a hazardous practice. Any undertaker with a few years under his or her belt will tell you that looks can certainly be deceiving. On the flip side of the coin, however, the same isn't so true. It's a one-way street.

The public *will* judge the business by the cover. The funeral ceremony, the funeral director, and the funeral home facility are all about image. Image is everything in this business. Can you imagine the undertaker showing up in the middle of the night at your house to take your mother wearing jeans and T-shirt? I know it's a ridiculous little example, but you'd probably slam the door in his or her face.

Perhaps one of the most essential parts of that image is the funeral home (or funeral parlor, chapel, or mortuary—whatever you call it). Managers and owners go to agonizing lengths to ensure the physical plant is as magnificent as it can possibly be. Funeral directors wear many hats, and one of them is part landscaper and part janitor. We spend a lot of our day making sure the grass is cut, leaves are raked, parlors are vacuumed, furniture is dusted, windows are cleaned, the trash cans are emptied, the cigarette butts are swept up, and the sidewalks are shoveled free of snow. It's the less glamorous aspect of the job, one they don't tell you about in mortuary school, but one of the most important.

Three generations ago, wakes were mainly held in the home. The undertaker would embalm the body in bed, and later bring the casket to the house* along with a giant zinc tub that he'd fill with ice and place the casket in. He'd bring folding chairs and the wake would proceed for several days. Early in the twentieth century there was a shift from the home to funeral parlors for preparation and viewing of the body, especially in urban areas. And the funeral directors wanted the families coming to the funeral parlor to feel as comfortable as possible, almost like they were at home. So they filled their businesses with antiques, plush carpeting, and rich draperies. Hence the obsession with perfection at the funeral home—it's almost like when you clean up before a big party at your house. To borrow another old term, you want to put your best foot forward. That's what we do; we create an atmosphere of the perfect home for the bereaved family. But unlike

---

*There are a lot of strange-looking cutouts in the entryway walls of old town homes; mostly they were put there on purpose to allow the casket to be brought into the house.

at home when your house is a wreck 360-some-odd days out of the year when you're not entertaining, we have to keep our best foot forward all year round.

By and large the decor of a funeral home isn't a thrilling subject. It's there. It looks nice. That's it. But this next story, about a couch, caught my eye. I've often looked at an antique and wondered about the previous owners, and the things that piece has "seen." This antique collector/funeral director certainly found out what his newest acquisition had witnessed.

Secret of the Settee
Contributed by an antique collector

I was at a high-end estate sale in Atlanta and found this fabulous Federal style settee. It was made out of fruitwood and covered in black-and-white wool damask with a pineapple carved at the crest of the seatback. It had to be at least 180 years old, all handmade, and appeared to be all original. If I could use one word to describe this piece: *divine*. The only tiny issue with the piece was a pink stain on the side.

I made a ridiculous offer, citing the stain as problematic, and the piece being hardly worth the offer I made. I acted like I was doing them a favor taking it off their hands. With the stain, the thing was practically worthless, or so I implied.

"We simply *couldn't* part with it for that," the haughty woman with big hair and half-moon glasses perched upon the end of her nose said upon hearing my offer.

I bid her good day, and wished her well in finding a buyer foolish enough to buy the damaged piece.

"Sir!" she called after me, the gold chain attached to her glasses jangling. "Perhaps we could come to an agreement."

She countered and I counter-countered, reminding her I

was doing her a favor by taking worthless trash off her hands. And the dance continued until she eventually accepted my original, laughable offer.

I hid my smile and triumphantly loaded my find into my pickup.

I know what you're thinking: "Wow, this guy is really gay." You're wrong, and I think my wife and three kids might even make an argument against you. I just have this thing for antiques.

I wasn't born an antique nut, and don't really even consider myself one today, but if I see a nice piece at a reasonable price I snap it up. You see, I have to meet certain expectations as the owner of a funeral parlor that other business owners don't have to meet.

Guests expect a certain level of decorum when going to a funeral home. It's a combination of copious amounts of wainscoting and trim, a calming color palette, fine draperies, soothing artwork, and of course, elegant furniture. You couldn't get away putting out that vulgar Ikea furniture you get when you go to a doctor's office in a funeral parlor. You show me a funeral director that makes you sit on vinyl and I'll show you someone who's about to go out of business. If I wanted to go sit on some vinyl sofa exploding stuffing and boasting cigarette burns I'd go to the nearest government building, not the place that's going to bury my mother. It's all about image, image, image.

I hope my minor furniture obsession now makes a little more sense for a straight man.

I have collected a lot of really nice antique furniture for my funeral parlor, but I'm bringing up this particular settee because I had the strangest encounter not too long ago.

The first calling time of the afternoon was winding down. The Hamilton family was going to go get some supper and come back to the funeral parlor for the next wave of well-

wishers peddling condolences unto them. Mr. Hamilton
sidled up to me in the foyer. He was a dandy-looking old
man, short and squatty with a great shock of white hair and
a three-piece suit that I'd guess dated back to the Carter
administration.

"We might not be here today if it wasn't for that couch,"
Mr. Hamilton said cryptically. I sometimes found him hard
to understand. He's from up North, New York I think, and
his speech is very clipped and tinny.

"What?" I said, loudly. I wasn't sure if I hadn't heard him
correctly or understood what he was saying.

He pointed at my prized settee with a gnarled finger
where his son, Martin, sat with his wife. "Fate. That's how
I ended up here because of that damn couch."

"Ended up where?" I said. I was totally confused.

"Georgia," he said and aimed the gnarled finger at me.
"I'm from North Jersey—Sinatra town. I was working for
the Central of Georgia Railroad. They were doing line
consolidations and things like that back then. It was good
pay for a boy. I saw a flier somewhere and came south on
the rails to see the country for a bit."

I had no idea what the railroad had to do with my settee
or him being in my parlor on this particular day, but his
filmy blue eyes had fixed me with such a hypnotic stare that
I nodded dumbly and said, "Okay."

"See, he doesn't know it," Mr. Hamilton said, nodding his
head toward Martin. He lowered his voice and beckoned me
down to his level, and putting his hand up as to shield our
voices up from Martin overhearing said, "but he was
conceived on that couch."

"Huh?" I said, now totally confused.

"Shh!" Mr. Hamilton scolded. "See, I met Millie when I
passed through Decatur. I met her at the social they used to
have in the park on Saturday nights; me and a couple of my

chums would sneak out of camp and go mix with the locals. Millie took a shine to me. Her parents didn't approve. I was a Yank, didn't belong. Back in those days our dates were chaperoned"—he wagged a finger in my face—"but one night we were left alone in the parlor of her parents house for a bit too long." He winked a rheumatic eye at me. "Nine months later, Martin was born."

I've sat on that settee! was all I could think, but my face remained expressionless though I raised an eyebrow.

"It was very scandalous back then, especially in the town Millie was from."

"I bet," I said, making a mental note never to sit on the settee again.

"Know what a shotgun wedding is?"

I nodded.

"Well, her daddy made sure he had a bead drawn on my back." He cackled. "But I didn't care. We were in love. Railroad crew moved on and I stayed here. Millie and I built a pretty good life." He removed the hand shield and straightened up. "Thing is, her daddy never really forgave her. Left the house to her sister. Sister married a wealthy man, and they didn't need for anything. They sold everything." He stared almost wistfully at the settee. "It dates to before the War."

There is only one *war* in the south—the one of Northern Aggression.

"It was Millie's daddy's granny's. Before then, who knows?" He shrugged.

I know antique furniture is a lot more unique than the crap they mass-produce today, but a thought had popped into my head. "How do you know that's the same couch? You haven't seen it in what, twenty years?"

He laughed and rubbed a hand over his face. "I reckon it's

been more like forty, but it's the same one. Gotta be, that black and white covering with a pineapple on top. But if you want to be sure, check the side there."

He pointed to the side I had butted up against the wall to hide the pink stain. "One Christmas shortly after we had married Millie was a little giddy and spilled a glass of red wine. And unless it's been recovered that wine stain will still be there."

"It's the same one," I mumbled. I was shocked, and must've looked so because Mr. Hamilton smiled as if he had already known it was the same one. *What are the odds?* I tried doing some quick calculations, but the odds seemed far too great, and quickly gave up.

"Isn't it strange," Mr. Hamilton said. "I'd likely be back in Jersey right now if it weren't for that couch, and our paths would've never crossed. But here I am with my family and my Millie laid out in your parlor and the reason for all that right here staring us in the face. It has a way of all working out, doesn't it?" He winked at me again and adjusted his suit jacket and turned his attention to the rest of his family that had trickled out of the viewing parlor "Come on now. Let's go get some supper."

I have seen and experienced a lot of strange and unusual things in this profession, but find it odd that the most unusual experience involves a piece of furniture. It's almost like my fate and Mr. Hamilton's and who-knows-who-else's are all balled and woven together like that wool fabric covering on that settee. I am a God-fearing man, and believe it was no accident that our paths collided on that particular occasion.

I'm convinced there are certain pivot points or crossroads that we come to in our lives that influence the trajectory—kind of a hybrid of the free will and predestination debate. Say, for example, you find yourself pointing a gun at someone. Shoot, and the chances are you'll predestine yourself to a long stretch of prison time. Lower the weapon and walk away, and who knows? That would be an example of a moment, standing at a major crossroads in life. I know the predestination camp would argue the path of whether or not you pull the trigger would be already set long before you get to that point, and the free will camp would argue that if you had pulled the trigger who says you'd be incarcerated? Perhaps it was self-defense.

That couch certainly didn't influence the course of Mr. Hamilton's life, but it was there, and certainly facilitated perhaps the largest crossroad he ever came to. If things had played out a little differently, he'd probably be back North, and the couch would probably still be in the family. Serendipitously, the piece of furniture that placed him there ends up in the funeral parlor where his wife was laid out.

Honestly though, what are the chances of that happening? Slim, but apparently not impossible.

Really, a chapter about furnishing a funeral home would be awful bland, and that previous story is about as wild as you can get when talking about the subject of furniture. This next story isn't necessarily about the furnishings as much as what was done with a furnishing to make for perhaps the oddest wake any of the well-wishers in the story would ever go to.

The idea in "The Big Easy" (opposite) isn't necessarily a novel idea, just very unorthodox. Some pictures circulated on the Internet recently depicting a gentleman from some country in South America who loved his crotch rocket (i.e., motorcycle) so much that when he died an untimely death the family requested he be viewed on the motorcycle. I have to hand it to those undertakers. They did a fine job. However they embalmed him to get him into a position so that it looked like he was riding his bike. They propped the bike up on Lucite stands, and put his helmet and leather jacket and riding gloves on and he looked good. So good that the photos showed up in my inbox, but that's not unusual—any joke, or anything of the morbid ilk, friends, family, and acquaintances feel the urge to automatically forward to me.

I've heard of, and seen, the dearly departed holding baseballs, cigarettes, rifles, golf clubs, assorted cups and mugs in repose, but "The Big Easy" takes all that to a whole different level. And of course, after I had heard this story, I received an email from another well-wisher with more photos that was very similar to this, but the dead man had a clicker in his hand, and the television on.

The Big Easy
Contributed by a camping enthusiast

The undertaker is the fly on the wall. We're omnipresent but seldom seen or heard. We blend into the background with our black suits, polished wingtips, starched white shirts, and muted ties (both in color and in pattern). I have, on occasion, seen my fellow brethren get really crazy and wear a small brass nameplate on the breast of their suit coat, but those are the rowdy ones. Me, I'm not that crazy; I'm your typical hovering, unseen force. And as the proverbial shadow, I hear *a lot* of things. I'm not talking about personal, confidential information entrusted to me by the families; I'm referring to miscellaneous comments and conversations made by people visiting the funeral home for a service.

Many times I have no idea what the conversation is about; I just hear these interesting little snippets. That wasn't the case not too long ago at a funeral. I heard plenty of snatches of conversation from visitors and knew exactly what they were about. It was one of those funerals (i.e., not traditional), and I expected to hear commentary. Take for example a husband and wife who showed up: he was dressed in a dark blue three-piece suit and she in a dress and fancy hat. After they signed the guest registry I directed them to the viewing parlor. As they entered the man leaned over to his wife and whispered none-too-softly, "Holy shit! Would you look at Cathy?"

The woman, obviously surprised herself judging by the look on her face, turned to the man and hissed, "Harry, language! We're in a funeral parlor; have some respect."

I chuckled a little. Everyone seemed a little startled as they entered the parlor, probably because they were expecting Mrs. Flint to be laid out in a casket and instead found her reclining comfortably in an easy chair.

Yes, an easy chair.

I got the death call for Mrs. Flint during supper. It was a lovely summer evening, and though late, it was still light enough that the neighborhood kids were still out riding their bikes. I called Marty, the apprentice, and had him meet me at the funeral home, and we rode over to Mrs. Flint's home in the funeral coach.

I knocked on the door and a woman with dirty blond hair about my age answered the door. I introduced myself and found out she was Cathy Flint's niece, Alex.

"Would you care to show me to your aunt?" I asked.

Alex guided me into the family room where Cathy Flint lay in a taupe-colored easy chair.

A girl, presumably Alex's daughter, sat on the sofa and held a growling mutt. "Can you shut Princess up?" Alex asked the girl. Her voice was taunt and warbly, like she was just keeping it together.

"I can't," the girl whined. "She won't settle down."

"Argh," Alex groaned and slapped her forehead. "That's Aunt Cathy's dog," she said to me, "I have no idea what we're going to do with her, because I can tell you my cats aren't going to get along well with her."

I smiled politely. I've heard that line in one form or another more times than I could count, and often wondered what became of those master-less pets. I already had three of my own, and my wife would crucify me if I brought any more home. I didn't take the growling personally. They all do it. They know what has happened and why I'm there. They instinctively know I'm there to take their master.

I said hello to the girl on the couch. Then, turning to Alex, said, "Okay, since the coroner's office has been notified, I'll be right in with Marty and my equipment."

Alex put a hand out and touched my shoulder, and then quickly withdrew like she was astonished that she had invaded my personal space. "Uh," she said, digging in her shorts, "you mind if I smoke?"

I wasn't sure why she asked, seeing as how she was already lighting it. "No, not at all," I lied.

Alex took that first deep lungful and looked at her daughter with a look like *here goes nothing*. "We have kind of an odd request."

I tried not to change my expression. "Oh?"

"Yeah. Aunt Cathy wanted a public visitation before being cremated, but didn't like confined spaces...like a coffin."

"No casket?"

"No. No coffin," she affirmed.

"Okay," I said. "If not a casket, then what did you have in mind?"

"Well..." She twisted her hair. "You're going to think me—her"—Alex gestured to her aunt—"odd, but she wanted to be laid out on that recliner." Inhale. Exhale. "Do you think that's odd?"

I frowned and lied. "A little unorthodox maybe, but it's certainly doable."

"Oh, thank God! Aunt Cathy always brought it up, but I never really gave it any thought until today and all this"— she motioned around the room with both hands— "was thrown in my lap by the neighbor calling and saying, 'Good morning Alex, I just keyed in and I think Cathy is dead.' Can you believe it? How the hell does 'good morning' preface that statement?"

I grinned in spite of myself. Some people don't even realize they're being humorous.

I assured her we'd be able to fulfill her aunt's wishes. Then I went out to the coach and prefaced my statement to Marty with "you're not going to believe this."

Over the years I've embalmed people in such a manner so that they can hold an item. The ones I can remember are a coffee cup, beer bottle, several cigarettes, and my favorite, the person flipping the bird. The embalming process essentially fixes the tissues in such a way that after embalming a person is "frozen" in a certain position. To achieve this, during the embalming a prosthesis is needed to hold the flaccid tissue in position until it fixates. For example, when I've gotten the requests for the decedent to be holding a cigarette I'll use a piece of a wooden dowel between the fingers, and then right before the visitation I'll insert the actual cigarette. I'm not going to go into details, but Mrs. Flint required a little more than a piece of a wooden dowel to position her properly so she'd look comfortable in her recliner.

The day after the next, Marty and I went over in my pickup truck and got the recliner from the house. This time, the pooch greeted me at the door, tail wagging and was all

too happy to sniff my dogs' scent on my shoes. I made
Marty do most of the moving and lifting while I stood
around and talked to Alex about details we hadn't covered
during the arrangement conference. "So, you don't think this
is too weird?" she kept asking.

"No," I said, only lying a little bit, "it's actually a
throwback to old times."

"Really?"

"Yeah, this was the way it was done a hundred years ago."

"They had recliners back then?"

I laughed. "No, but people were laid out and viewed in
their beds. It was common practice. This is the same
concept."

She smiled. I could tell she liked it. "Yeah, I guess it is. You
want a soda?"

"I'd love one. Marty," I called. He was red faced, and
huffing trying to hoss the recliner into the pickup by himself.
"You want something cold to drink?"

He stopped lifting and tried to catch his breath. I
wouldn't use the adjectives *thin, trim,* or *in shape* in any
sentence describing Marty (not that I am any of those things
either, but I have an excuse: thirty years on him), and this bit
of exertion was taking its toll on him. "Yeah, that'd be great."
He wiped his beet-red face with his shirttail.

"Okay, when I come back out, we'll go."

He pointed to the recliner but I pretended not to notice.

Inside, I quaffed the ice-cold Coke and continued, "Yeah,
in fact, there used to be a bed at the funeral home. It was
just a twin bed that we'd knock together real quick for a
private family viewing. We never used it for a public viewing
to my knowledge, but a couple of generations ago it wasn't
uncommon for people to pay their respects at a house and
the deceased was still in bed. In fact, I think it's still a
common practice in some European countries."

"Well, this really puts my mind at ease," Alex said and fired up another cigarette. "Oh, damn!"

"What?"

She held up a Coke can and made an "oops" face. "I don't have any more cold ones. All I have are room temperature."

I waved my hand and replied, "Ah, Marty won't mind." I drained my refreshingly cold Coke and went out to roust Marty, whom I found slumped over the fender of my truck. "Come, old boy," I said, slapping his shoulders, "wake up, you're driving us back."

He groaned.

"Oh don't fuss, I got you a Coke."

Two days later I finalized the arrangement of floral tributes around the taupe-colored recliner. Mrs. Flint looked quite good, albeit curious, I decided. I adjusted the volume of the music, adjusted the lighting, and went and unlocked the doors for the viewing.

No matter what you're expecting, wherever you go just remember: the unexpected can happen in any situation. Always remember the collection of sympathy peddlers who congregated expecting to find Cathy Flint laid out in a velvet-lined box, hands crossed over chest, but instead found her reared back comfortably in her easy chair.

CHAPTER 13

Epitaph

*Our dead are never dead to us, until we have
forgotten them.*

—GEORGE ELIOT

I guess it's fitting for my profession, but I love reading headstones. And as you can imagine I'm in various cemeteries almost every day, so I read a lot of monuments during the course of a year. I like to stare at the names and dates and wonder what that person was like and what kind of life they led. Unfortunately, there isn't a lot that can be gleaned from just a name and two dates. Sometimes, however, if I'm lucky, there'll be a bit more than just the standard name and dates, and that gives me a little thrill. I love the personalized monument, so I was thrilled when my neighbor, Clara Gallop, pushed the contemporary boundaries and went for a little personalization.

Ben Franklin once said, "Show me your cemeteries, and I will tell you what kind of people you have." He was referring to something that I see as almost a lost art: the prose of the epitaph. An epitaph is an inscription on a monument that tells a little something about the person buried there. Epitaphs were popular during Ben's time, and well through the nineteenth century, oftentimes accompanied by a skull and crossbones. Ben's monument inscription reads like a mini-novel, fitting for a printer.

I don't sell too many monuments, but when I do it's generally the same: name, date. Different stone, but still name, date. We're just a name, date society. In two hundred years when a young man or woman walks through the cemetery of our generation resting peacefully they will know nothing of who we were, what we stood for, or what struggles we endured. All they'll see is a name and date. I'm not saying people have to put something clever or pithy; I'm saying just make sure you're memorialized in a way that is fitting to your life. For example, the great American writer F. Scott Fitzgerald's epitaph is emotive, yet simple. It reads:

SO WE BEAT ON, BOATS AGAINST
THE CURRENT, BORNE BACK
CEASELESSLY INTO THE PAST.

That is a quote from his masterpiece *The Great Gatsby*. The beauty of that inscription is that even if you are someone who has never read a single sentence composed by F. Scott, or knows he was a novelist, by reading the tablet you'd know instinctively *what* he was.

Contrastingly, a man named Lester Moore had something a little less traditional (and certainly a bit wittier) inscribed on his stone. Lester was a station agent for Wells Fargo and is buried in Boot Hill Cemetery in Tombstone, Arizona, the famous cowboy town immortalized by countless films.

HERE LIES LESTER MOORE
FOUR SLUGS FROM A .44
NO LES NO MORE

And of course there are the more ironic epitaphs like B. Pearl Roberts in the 1847 Key West Cemetery. Roberts was noted by the locals as a hypochondriac whose epitaph reads I TOLD YOU I WAS SICK, and Ellen Shannon who lies in Girard Cemetery in Pennsylvania:

IN MEMORY OF
ELLEN SHANNON
AGE 26 YEARS
WHO WAS FATALLY
BURNED MAR. 21, 1870
BY THE EXPLOSION
OF A LAMP FILLED
WITH R. E. DANFORTH'S
NON EXPLOSIVE
BURNING FLUID

And then there's this famous workingman's "epitaph" that was buried in the hands of Grandpa Joad—along with some scripture—in *The Grapes of Wrath*. I use quotations because it's more of a literary epitaph than a literal one.

THIS HERE IS WILLIAM JAMES JOAD, DYED OF A STROKE, OLD
OLD MAN. HIS FOKES BURED HIM BECAWS THEY GOT NO
MONEY TO PAY FOR FUNERLS. NOBODY KILT HIM. JUS A STROKE
AND HE DYED

Serious, amusing, or ironic, an epitaph is a lasting memorial of the person in repose beneath the monument. When all your friends and family are long dead, it's how you will be remembered for posterity. Most of us will only be remembered as a name and two dates separated by a dash. Clara Gallop was the first person I encountered who wasn't a name, date kind of gal. Then again, while she was alive, she was larger than life, so shouldn't she be in death?

I moved in next door to Clara Gallop when I was in my late thirties. During the three years we lived next to each other we became quite good friends. Clara was the original owner of the house, had been there forty-seven years. During that time she had seen nine different presidents in office, the Beatles storm America, the USSR fall, twelve grandchildren and three great-grandchildren born, and had gone through three husbands. She had big hair, a big Lincoln Towncar that was as long as a space shuttle, and a personality that was even bigger.

The day after I moved in there was a knock on the door. I opened it to find a woman with big hair and a loud-patterned dress on my front step.

"Hi," the woman said, thrusting her hand out. "I'm your next door neighbor, Clara Gallop." She paused and pointed to the right to indicate exactly which neighbor she was. "Welcome to the neighborhood!"

"Thank you," I said. "Name's Ken."

"Would you care to come over for a highball this afternoon?"

I had no idea what the hell a *highball* was, but accepted and later that afternoon found myself and my partner on her back veranda, next to the koi pond drinking an old-fashioned cocktail. If you don't know what an old-fashioned is it's pretty much like drinking straight bourbon. Clara—who nearly had a fit when I called her Mrs. Gallop—told us all the neighborhood gossip, about her life and her family, and of course, her pride and joy, her yard. It was a beautifully maintained yard filled with all sorts of shrubs, trees, and flowerbeds. I had assumed it was professionally maintained. I was right, but it was Clara who professionally maintained it.

Clara told us between puffs from a 100 cigarette that she had gotten a horticulture certification, "back in the days when most women didn't go to college." We sipped the strong drinks as Clara walked us around the yard telling us about all the different gardens she had maintained over her career, but her home garden was her "pet project," as she called it.

"Been part of the garden tour for the past forty years; only missed one year," she told us proudly.

I couldn't believe an eighty-nine-year-old woman could keep such an immaculate yard. There wasn't a weed in sight, all of the shrubs were perfectly shaped, and every blade of grass seemed to be perfectly straight.

My partner, who can hold his booze pretty well, tapped out after two, and staggered home to lie down. Later, as Clara poured her fourth, she asked, "Ken, would you like a refresher?" I was a little cross-eyed, but accepted, and nearly blanched as she refilled it up to the brim. "So let me tell you the names of my koi—" And she was off and running. It was dark when I finally swam home.

A couple of weeks after my first visit with Clara, I was on my way home from a burial when I stopped at home to have dinner before a nighttime visitation. Clara was on all fours in a flowerbed when I pulled up in the hearse.

She shaded her eyes against the brim of her floppy hat. "What, are you some sort of undertaker or something?"

I tugged at the knot in my tie, loosening it. "Something like that."

"I never would've guessed in a million years!" she said, cackling. She pushed herself up and moseyed over to my driveway, wiping dirt from her gardening gloves. "You're too young and good-looking to be an undertaker."

"You think we're all old and dour?"

"Never met one that wasn't. You sure as hell can't drink like one." Clara cackled at her joke. "My second husband was good friends with an undertaker. Let me tell you, that man could drink like a fish!" She pulled off her gardening gloves and pulled out one of her long cigarettes from her apron, lit it, and said, "I'm working on quitting. I'm down to half a pack a day."

She had told me the joke a few weeks prior. "Congratulations," I said, waited for the punch line.

"Been a down to a half a pack for twenty years." She cackled again.

I laughed politely like I hadn't heard it before.

"You know something?" she asked. Without waiting for a reply she continued, "I've got this little saying. Every time anyone asks me how I'm doing, I always reply, 'Not pushing daisies.' Get it? Me, being a horticulturalist."

"I get it."

"Now I'm living next to an undertaker. Who would've thought!"

She walked away muttering the ironies of the universe to herself and cackling.

I went in for dinner.

Over the next three years when I would pull up in the driveway Clara would wave from wherever she was working in the yard and say, "Hi, undertaker."

"Hi, Clara," I'd reply. "How are you?"

"Not pushing daisies," she'd reply.

Then we'd both chuckle.

Occasionally she'd have my partner and me over for a highball and hold us hostage until we were good and liquored up. "Ship can't sail with only one mast," she'd say over our objections while refilling our tumblers. She baked us cookies at Christmas and brought us over pots of tulips at Easter. Clara Gallop was just an all-around good neighbor.

Three years later when the flowers started to bloom, Clara was conspicuously absent from her prized yard. I went over to inquire and found out she was gravely ill. She was ill enough to be in a nursing home, but she refused to leave her house. Clara directed her children to have the hospital bed set up beside the French doors so she could look outside to her garden. Clara's eldest daughter, Dee, invited me in, and I found a shriveled form huddled beneath the blankets piled on the hospital bed.

"Hi, undertaker," a weak voice beneath the mound said.

"How you feeling?" I sat on the edge of the bed and patted the gray hand resting on the brightly patterned blanket.

"Not pushing daisies," she replied.

We both smiled, but mine was a sad smile. I knew the end was near.

It wasn't too many more nights after my visit that I received a call. It was Dee. Clara had died.

I performed my job in preparing the body, and arranged for a wonderful ceremony: in Clara's backyard, amongst the trees, plants, and flowers she had so lovingly coaxed along. We buried her between two of her husbands, and a few weeks after the funeral I called Dee about inscribing her name on the stone at the cemetery.

"I've been thinking about it," she admitted. "My mom was such a . . . force."

"Oh yes, that she was," I agreed. "I'm down to half a pack a day," I said.

"Been a down to a half a pack for twenty years," Dee replied.

We both laughed.

"I wanted to put something on the stone to commemorate her, but couldn't come up with anything, and lo and behold when I was going through her papers the other day I found what she wants inscribed on her stone." She hesitated like she wasn't sure. "Let me know what you think; it's kind of macabre."

"Nothing your mother could do would shock me," I assured her.

She took a deep breath like she wasn't sure and said, "Pushing daisies."

It caught me completely off guard. I laughed out loud. "I love it!"

Dee laughed a nervous laugh of relief. "You think so?"

"Are we talking about the same woman here? Of course!" I caught myself and changed my voice to more professional tone I use for people I don't know that well. "But if you think it's a bit too much ... think about it. The choice is ultimately yours. I don't want you to do something you'll regret."

"No, no, you're right," Dee said, her voice getting stronger. "That was my mother. Her life was one of botanical pursuit and with her attitude, I think those two words sum her up perfectly." She laughed a surprised laugh. "See, even in death Clara knows best!"

I agreed to make up an engraving order and mail it to her, and told her that if she changed her mind we had plenty of time to do it.

She didn't change her mind and Clara Gallop is now pushing daisies. I think it's a fitting epitaph.

I haven't decided what my epitaph will read, but I know for sure I'm not just going to be a name, date. I will have lived a life and will not allow myself to be boiled down to a name and two dates separated by a dash.

Don't allow yourself to be a name, date either; your life matters. Be remembered; because you too will one day be pushing daisies.

Variations of this message have been immortalized on count-less headstones as a "popular" epitaph (if there is such a thing):

REMEMBER, MAN, AS YOU WALK BY

AS YOU ARE NOW, SO ONCE WAS I,

AS I AM NOW, SO SHALL YOU BE

REMEMBER THIS AND FOLLOW ME.

It's a sobering reminder that the days are long, but the years short.

CHAPTER 14

Raising the Roof

I wasn't sure whether to laugh or cringe when I heard Vinnie's story. Because, though amusing, I've had an apple out of Vinnie's barrel. But whereas Vinnie was an innocent bystander, I was the culprit.

I was in the funeral home's parking lot after my little saga went down. I didn't want to dial the phone, but I had no choice. I had fucked up. Big time.

The person on the other end of the phone line picked up. "Hello?"

"Uh, Uncle?"

"Hey, how'd the move go?" he asked.

"Well, here's the thing…" I paused for a long time. "I'm at the funeral home right now… with the state police. There's, uh, been"—I searched for the right word—"an incident."

That's the conversation that ended my moving day. And by "moving day" I mean the type where you call all your friends and con them into coming over to your house and helping you pack up all your stuff and move it from one dwelling to the next. Nothing to do with funerals, the dead, the bereaved, or the like, but somehow my moving day ended at the funeral home with a Statie and me on the phone, hat in hand, to Uncle Rick.

The day started off well enough. I had the bright idea of saving money by *not* hiring a moving company, and renting the truck myself and enlisting the help of friends and family members for the move. So I scampered on down to the rental office bright and early to pick up the nineteen footer I had reserved. When I was filling out the paperwork the clerk asked me, "Mr. Harra, would you like to buy the additional insurance?"

I thought about it for a moment. The cost of the insurance was more than the cost of the rental for the day, but I'm by no means a professional driver, so I replied, "Sure." And took the keys and drove off with walk-away insurance, or so I thought.

I bought coffee and doughnuts and by the time I arrived back at the town house the crew was assembled. It was early March in Delaware—when the weather can be very uncertain—but it was going to be a beautiful day to move, sunny and reasonably warm. I fed and watered the workers and we got to work. My wife and I lived in a glorified dollhouse and in no time we had the truck jammed with all our worldly possessions. It was going to be a single-trip move.

A cortège of cars (a reference to a funeral procession) left the city and followed the moving truck to our new house in the suburbs, and in just a few short hours we had everything unloaded. I left everyone under the direction of my wife to move items around while a few of us went to my parents' house to pick up a few items they had been storing in their basement for us, and we successfully transported them back to our new digs. The truck was a lot bigger than what I was used to (even a hearse, which is surprisingly easy to maneuver, but as I would learn later, *much* lower), but I was getting comfortable with it.

When we got back with the load from my parents' house my wife and her soldiers had started amassing a pile of junk left by the former owners: carpeting, boxes, old window treatments, odds and ends from the basement, and the like. They had created this huge mound of trash in the garage.

I hadn't yet signed up for residential trash pickup, and didn't know even if they would take the mountain of junk. But my mom had a bright idea: "Why don't you go throw that stuff in the funeral home Dumpster?"

Brilliant.

We loaded that moving truck like a trash truck and my dad hopped in to help me unload it at the funeral home. It is only a mile's ride and I pulled into the main entrance in no time. Now mind you, I come flying in and out of this main drive half a dozen or more times in a day, every day of the year, so I just turned the corner and gunned it. My dad and I were busy chatting away when all the sudden he pushed against the dash and yelled, "Oh sh—!"

The rest didn't come out. It was replaced by the sound of the roof of the truck ripping off like the lid of a sardine can.

The height of the porte cochere was about ten foot six inches.

The height of the truck was a good foot over that—or it had been, before I ripped it clean off.

A colleague of mine, who was meeting with a family, came racing out the front door and, not immediately recognizing me because I wasn't in the suit he normally saw me in and a watch cap obscured my head, yelled, "Hey! What the—" Then, realizing it was me, said in an *I'm telling* tone a child might use, "What have you done?"

The dust was still settling around the scene as I got out to inspect the damage. There was smashed wood, from the truck and building, everywhere, and rocks strewn all over the parking lot.

The rocks were from the roof. It is a roofing system that is a rubber membrane with river rocks laid out over them. Some rocks were as far as one hundred feet from the roof. My colleague later confirmed that rocks were flying by the window of the office he was in, a good clip down the building. And these were good-sized rocks, the size of a man's fist or bigger. I had hit the building *hard*.

All I could think was: *What an asshole I am!*

According to the rental insurance papers I had to file a police report, and thus came the red and blue flashing lights and the humble phone call to my uncle. To his credit, he began to laugh as I outlined "the incident."

The rental agency was closed when I went to return the truck, but I didn't want to void the rental agreement and subsequently void the insurance supplement, so I dropped it off (no roof and all), just like the contract stated.

I received a phone call on Monday. "Uh, Mr. Harra?" There was a pregnant silence from the guy on the other end. "Looks like you had a problem over the weekend."

Yes, I did.

"How will you be covering the damages?"

"What are you talking about? I got the extra insurance."

There was another long pause.

Turns out the fine print didn't cover the "box" or whatever they called the thing I tore off. After reading the fine print, the insurance didn't cover much of anything. I'd have been better covered if I had went to a soothsayer and paid $50 to protect me from bad luck, or, in my case, idiocy.

The move ended up costing me a lot more than if I had quit being so cheap and bucked up for a moving company. But I guess I should just be glad things didn't turn out as bad for me as they did for Vinnie.

Altar Call to a Car
Contributed by a basement beer brewer

One of the nice things about my profession are the thank-you cards. I think it's a unique phenomenon that only happens in my profession, to receive a thank-you card. I mean, honestly, when was the last time you sent a card to your lawyer saying, "Thank you, John Doe, Esquire, for writing such a nuanced will!" or to your doctor, "Thank you, Dr. Smith, for lancing that nasty boil off my foot!"? You don't.

Those little squares of paperboard, sometimes with a gaudy design on the front, and always handwritten, are a tangible reminder of why I do this job. I have a steamer trunk in my study at home where I toss the cards. When it has been an especially tough day, I'll lift the lid as if to reassure myself, that, yes, I have made a difference. The most recent card I received was certainly nondescript but by far the most memorable. It was just a plain white card with a purple flower on the front and "thank you" printed in script. Inside it said: *Vinnie, Thank you for providing such a memorable service for mother.—Lorraine*

Seems like a run-of-the-mill card, right? Maybe the words are, but the funeral those words belie was anything but.

Lorraine Powell came in with her brother Ben and her aging father, Mr. Powell, to make funeral arrangements. Mr. Powell was hard of hearing, and a stroke had left him a little confused, so Lorraine and Ben made most of the arrangements, asking their father periodically if he was in agreement. Mr. Powell, a sweet old guy, agreed with whatever Lorraine and her brother yelled into his ear. Everything was fine with him.

Lorraine and Ben chose a nice maple wood casket with a light blue interior to match the burial dress they brought in.

They selected flower arrangements, a stationery package, and together we composed a nice death notice for the newspaper. Because of their father's advancing age, Lorraine and Ben didn't want to spread the funeral services over two days the traditional way with a viewing in the evening and services the next day. But they did like the old way of the evening calling hours, so people didn't have to take off work. So I suggested an evening viewing followed by a service that night, and then the following day Ben, Lorraine, the minister, and myself could go to the cemetery for a brief interment service. They liked that idea.

Three days later, the three of them arrived for the visitation. It was about two weeks before Christmas, and was already twilight when Ben and Lorraine escorted their unsteady father up the walk. I had salted the walk, a common precaution in Northern Ohio in the wintertime.

I gathered their coats and let them spend some time with Mrs. Powell before their guests began arriving. Mr. Powell sat at the head of the casket in a chair and did his best to keep up with the stream of visitors that came to pay their respects.

Mr. and Mrs. Powell had worked their whole lives, he in a cannery, and she as a checker in a grocery store. They had lived in the area for their entire lives and had been very active in the their church and other organizations. As a result, there were a lot of people in the community who wanted to come pay their respects as well as friends and schoolmates of Lorraine's and Ben's. When it was time to seat everyone for the service the parlor was full.

The minister, an evangelist I call Rodney Dangerfield behind his back, began what promised to be one of his usual long-winded sermons. I sat in the lobby and ushered late-arriving guests into the parlor. After some scripture and prayer I ducked into the parlor and cued up a hymn on the CD player.

"Now," Rodney said, once the song had ended, "we're going to have Lorraine come up and offer a few words of remembrance about her mother and then we're going to open up the floor for testimonials." He shuffled back to his seat behind the podium and sat. I refer to him as Rodney because he looks like the late comedian and grins a lot, not because of his personality. I think fake Rodney would faint dead at the mere *thought* of a four-letter word.

Lorraine came up and offered a very nice eulogy with a couple vignettes at the end designed to be humorous, but were only so in the context of the funeral. The crowd laughed politely. Afterward, Pastor Dangerfield pranced around the room offering the microphone to anyone who wanted to speak a few words about Mrs. Powell.

Then he began his sermon. Rodney is like a computer booting up. He starts off slow, but by the time he is up and running and the central processor is firing on all microchips there's no stopping him. When he finally ran out of gas I could tell the crowd was bored. I played another hymn and it was almost time to wrap things up, but Rodney had one more item on his agenda, an altar call. This is the point in the service where he tries to convert any nonbelievers.

"Friends," Rodney said, "If there is anyone out in the audience tonight who doesn't know the love of Jesus Christ I ask you to accept him into your heart now and are welcomed into His everlasting kingdom in heaven." He pounded his closed Bible on the podium, ready to offer further evidence to elicit a decision from any still dubious in the audience. "The Apostle Paul said, 'I came declaring the message of God about Jesus Christ, confidently relying on the Holy Spirit powerfully to take that message and make it effective—'"

What happened next, what interrupted Rodney, I can best describe it as an airplane crashing into the building, at least that's what it felt like. The funeral home is an all-brick building that used to be a bank, so it's very sturdy. But there was a loud explosion followed by the building actually quaking. Ceiling tiles fell out of the ceiling onto the assembled crowd, lamps fell off tables, and the power flickered. Above the screams of the crowd I hear Rodney shout "Holy Jesus!" His arms flung up like he was accepting the rapture from above.

I raced into the lobby and there I saw the steaming grill of a car poking through a wall! Drywall and bricks were strewn about the lobby like a bomb had gone off. I raced outside to find the tail end of an enormous Cadillac with a little old lady getting out.

"Hold it!" I said. "Don't move, you may be hurt."

She ignored me and got out. The woman couldn't have been taller than four feet and was wearing a full-length fur coat that kind of made her look like a gorilla and a pillbox hat. Looking confused, she turned to me and said, "Oh, my, did I do that?"

"Yeah," I said miserably, looking at my destroyed funeral home, guests streaming, some screaming, out the front door in exodus.

The police preliminarily thought the woman had hit a patch of black ice and lost control while keeping her foot firmly planted on the accelerator. She jumped the curb off the highway, crossed a strip of grass, miraculously missed the business sign, then crossed the single drive in front of the funeral home, and somehow jumped another curb before driving through a flower bed and ultimately plowing through the lobby wall. With all those horses and all those tons of metal in those older Cadillacs it was like having a miniature Sherman tank hit the funeral home.

Pastor Dangerfield made a point to seek me out before he left. "Pretty powerful stuff, huh?"

I glared at him. I wasn't in the mood.

He held up his hands in a defensive gesture. "Might take a day or two for you to see the big picture." I could see the excitement in his eyes: he had sermon material for the next five years. He was pumped. "But hey," he clapped me on the back. "Could've been worse, Vin. You could've been sitting in that lobby like you normally do. If that were the case..." He trailed off. We both knew what he meant. I'd be dead.

"Thanks," I said somewhat more sarcastically than I'd meant, but I wasn't in the mood for appeasements.

He tapped his head. "Think about it."

I arrived home that night bone cold because the firefighters wouldn't let anyone back into the building because they were worried about structural issues, so I had to stand out in the frigid temperatures and see that everyone left in an orderly manner. I poured myself a stiff cognac and let the liquor warm my insides.

"Tough night?" my wife asked, noting the drink.

"Some woman lost her driver's license tonight."

"What?" she said, hands on hips because she thought I was using some metaphor.

"Really," I said, taking another sip of the amber liquid, "some woman drove her car into the funeral home during the service. I'm sure she'll lose her license."

Rebecca put her hand over her mouth. "No!"

"Oh, yeah," I said, tossing the rest of cognac back. "What a night."

"Literally through the funeral home?"

"Her car is parked in the lobby." I was being facetious. It had been towed.

"My God! How is the funeral home?"

"Not too good."

"I might join you," she said referring to the drink. Her face looked a little pale.

Two days later, once my funeral home had been deemed safe to enter, I was sitting in my office when the phone rang. It was Lorraine.

I thought she would want to talk about the rescheduling of her mother's burial; no, she wanted to talk about the altar call.

"Wasn't it amazing that at the exact moment Preacher said the Holy Spirit would..." she prattled on. I, only half listening, agreed with all the miracles she conjured up. I was up to my ears in insurance, engineers, construction companies, and everything else, not to mention my normal business I was trying to conduct. Eventually I was able to nail her down about a burial date.

I finally buried Mrs. Powell, and a day before Christmas received a thank-you note from Lorraine. It was brief, but it said a lot. I included the newspaper clipping of the accident in the card and threw it in the trunk with the others.

There's that old saying, lightning never strikes the same place twice. Vinnie better hope that holds true, because Rodney Dangerfield might just bring the rapture next time and bring a coach bus through his chapel. I'm worried about the whole lightning thing because six months after I tore the roof off the moving truck lightning didn't strike, but a chocolate truck did.

I was on the phone with a colleague at our other funeral home when all the sudden he yelled, "Oh sh—!" and the line went dead. I called back but there was no answer. Nor was there an answer twenty minutes later. I found out the reason why when I got in my car and went to investigate.

Firemen and police officers milled about the front drive, and there was a big chocolate truck with two metal I-beams sitting on top of the box, surrounded by hundreds of bricks. They were everywhere, on the lawn, in the drive, in the flowerbeds, *everywhere*. The driver of the chocolate truck had hit the porte cochere going so fast the supporting walls, made out of bricks, literally exploded.

Suddenly, I didn't feel like such a jerk. The bulk of the damage I did was to the truck. At least I didn't tear a good portion of the building down—in a chocolate truck no less.

CHAPTER 15

The Gift

*Let us so live that when we come to die even the
undertaker will be sorry.*

—MARK TWAIN

I stated earlier, in "The Label: Undertaker," that the dead
only have the memories left of them. That's only partially true. In the metaphysical sense it's a possession
(perhaps their only) of the dead, the knowledge that their memory will live on: the linking of the living and dead. But in the
physical sense the dead don't have any real possessions. There
are cemeteries filled with "rich" dead men and women.

One can spend a lifetime of acquiring money, property, possessions, or you name it—anything that can be acquired and collected. In the time it takes to snap your fingers that dearly
departed is just as wealthy as the next (calling to mind the old
axiom, you can't take *any* of it with you).

But we can cultivate perpetual memories and continue our
work, when dead, through our legacy. Essentially, the one thing
you *can* take with you is the knowledge that the memories of you
will live through your legacy. In the most literal sense a legacy
would be money or property, but it can also be something a lot
more valuable and unforgettable like morals, philosophies, or

traditions. Webster's second definition of legacy is "anything handed down from the past, as from an ancestor, or predecessor."

Anything.

You can leave anything as your legacy.

And I argue that "anything" can be a more significant legacy than something as trite as money.

I'll give you an example. My grandparents left me an "anything" legacy.

When my grandfather, a young captain in the United States Army, combat veteran, and Bronze Star recipient, was riding a troop transport train home at the end of the Second World War, the train stopped unexpectedly in Williamsburg, VA. Typical of the postwar chaos associated with thousands of servicemen trying to get home, the train was stopped for hours without reason. It just so happened his car was right behind the recently rebuilt Governor's Palace. The Governor's Palace is the grandest of all the buildings in John Rockefeller's rebuilt colonial town. And Bob, sitting there staring at this impressive, peculiar building, decided he wanted to come back and visit with his wife on vacation.

They returned several times during the next several decades, and enjoyed it so much that they decided they would begin bringing their three young boys there every year during the Christmas season. As the years progressed, the boys grew up, got married, had children, and those children had children. The family continued to reconvene every year in Williamsburg around the same time for a family reunion, even after their parents died.

So you see, though they both are long dead, their tradition—their legacy—lives on. The candles in the windows, the pine roping, and colonial sprays on the tavern doors evoke memories of them, but it's not just the memories. It's also the values of family and togetherness in their legacy that lives, and keeps their memories alive and vibrant. It's a legacy that I will pass on down to my children.

Many times a person's legacy can shine through their occupational work. Look at the example of Steve Jobs. He will forever be remembered for all his technological contributions. But there are millions of other humbler contributions made daily around the world. I know a woman whose grandfather was an Italian stonemason. He was the old-school type of stonemason who worked well into his eighties; a small sprite of a man but with forearms the size of ham hocks who could heft small boulders with a single hand. Every time she drives past the church he built, a giant stone goliath, she thinks of him. That's his legacy he left for her and the world.

The DuPont Company is headquartered in Wilmington, and over the years it enticed the brightest and best minds to the area to invent and work for them. It's a common occurrence for a family to ask me to include in an obituary that *John Smith* held thirty patents. In fact, every time I pass a house under construction, wrapped in Tyvek, I think of my grandfather, Max, who contributed to the invention of that product. It's certainly not as sexy as a giant stone church, but in a sense it's my stone church.

Robert H. Jackson, Supreme Court justice, said, "Your job today tells me nothing of your future—your use of your leisure today tells me just what your tomorrow will be." Essentially what the Honorable Jackson is saying is that your gifts don't have to be occupational; they are oft revealed in the form of someone's hobby. And it doesn't have to be a traditional "hobby," it can be that indefinable *anything*: music, carpentry, poetry, food, establishing traditions, doing charitable work or acts, or a myriad of other tangible or intangible skills an individual has to offer.

I have had more than several different families bring in cassette tapes of music because their mom or dad was a pianist or flautist or horn player, either solo or in a band, and this is their parent's legacy to them: the gift of music. I play the tapes during the viewings and sometimes during the service, when the family wants to have a song of reflection. Those tapes and CDs remind me of my cousin's legacy. Esther was a second cousin (maybe once removed) of mine, who was so gifted at the piano when she was young girl, the piano teacher told her mother after the first lesson, "There is nothing I can teach her. Her skill level is far above anyone's I have ever seen...even mine!" Esther never took another lesson in her life. She could listen to any song and replay it perfectly, and remember it forever. Even as advanced age took her mind, she could still sit down at a piano and play effortlessly for hours. Though I can't tickle the ivories myself, every time I hear piano music I think of her. Through that Esther will never die.

Regardless if it is tangible or intangible, we all have gifts to offer to the world. I really liked this story because it illustrates how one man established a legacy that ensured his memory would live on in the minds of thousands of people.

If you don't think you have a gift to offer the world, hopefully Thomas Bleek will change your mind.

Different Shoes
Contributed by a blogger

Thomas Bleek lived to be almost a hundred. Unlike the name suggests his life was anything but bleak. Thomas, the son of poor Welsh immigrants, seized the American dream and never let go. He sucked the marrow from life and let the juices drip joyfully down his chin.

Thomas attended Princeton on a scholarship where he played basketball and football. He studied law at Boston

University, and then played pro ball for the Boston Redskins and later the Shamrocks. In those days, the thirties, professional football wasn't a full-time job; Thomas was a lawyer by profession and football player by heart. He joined the service when the second Great War broke out, and served in the JAG Corps in the European theater.

We had Thomas's service in a fire hall because no church, and certainly my funeral home, could accommodate the number of people that was expected to turn out to pay their respects. Thomas was laid out at the front of the hall in a steel casket, black because it is the color of a judge's robe. The floral tributes stretched from one end of the room to the other. The receiving family members looked like they were standing in a jungle. The fireman's band insisted on playing for the entire wake. Thomas had donated a lot of money to their cause over the years, and though they were looking at four straight hours of jamming, they insisted on doing it. Right at eight o'clock I cued the band, and threw open the fire hall doors to the waiting crowd.

It was a crisp February morning, the kind where the air fairly snaps and it is just overcast enough to cast a gunmetal-gray pallor on everything—the perfect day for a funeral. My associates and I had trouble keeping all the well-wishers from standing out in the cold. There was simply no place for all the people to go. The line was long and never died down during the four-hour calling time, though the children and grandchildren (Mrs. Bleek had died years ago) did a good job of not talking too much to any one person, and thus keeping the line moving. I know there were at least a thousand who went through the line because we ran out of the eight hundred prayer cards a good hour before service time.

Service time came and went and still the line was strong. After another hour, with no end in sight, Mr. Bleek's son, a mere spring chick of seventy-seven, had had enough of small talk.

I agreed. He had been greeting people for five hours and that would exhaust someone my age. I cut the line off. Of course there was the usual outrage, but sometimes cutting the line is the only thing we can do in situations like this. And that's what you pay me for, among other things, to be your bagman.

Thomas Bleek, according to what his family told me, wasn't a very religious man, but was deeply spiritual. So I arranged for a funeral celebrant, rather than a member of the clergy, to officiate his funeral. A funeral celebrant is someone certified in performing a secular service that focuses on the individual's life rather than the liturgy that a religious service will follow. I thought it to be the perfect fit for a man who had led such a rich life.

Pamela, the celebrant, took my cue when I introduced her and teetered up to the podium. She was relatively new to doing celebrant services, and a crowd this size cowed her a bit. She looked out across the sea of faces and gripped the podium. The fire hall had three hundred folding chairs. I had ordered a matching amount from a party supplier, and still the hall was *beyond* standing room only. It was packed to the gills. I settled into my place next to a sign posted on the wall that read: BY ORDER OF THE FIRE MARSHALL, MAXIMUM OCCUPANCY 550 PERSONS.

Pamela drew a ragged breath and launched into her service. "Welcome everybody. We're here today to celebrate the life of a community leader, family man, patriot, and all around great guy. I encourage each of you to look around and see all the lives Thomas touched."

Heads turned, and indeed there were a lot of disparate people. Which is strange for a funeral. Generally you get people of a similar socioeconomic status of the deceased—

because that's who were in that person's circle of friends. But not Thomas Bleek. Looking around I saw young men and women wearing thousand-dollar suits sitting next to people who looked like they lived on the street. No matter the person, rich or poor, they all sat in rapt attention and listened to Pamela's story of Thomas's life. Her voice slowly grew stronger as she realized she had the attention of the audience.

Pamela told of Thomas's appointment as a judge, and his weekly football column he wrote for the newspaper until he was ninety-one. She spoke about his love of gardening, and how he boasted the best lawn in his neighborhood and how his neighbors were never without a bag of fresh produce hanging from their doorknobs, and of course who could forget his monthly, half-hour radio show on gardening? Pamela also talked about his charity work, something *he* never spoke of: the men's shelter, soup kitchen, adult literacy program, and a lot more that I can't even remember.

"Funny thing is," Pamela said, "I wasn't sure until this morning how I would conclude such an amazing life. How do you sum something like that up?"

She spread her hands and panned the audience. She knew she had them eating out the palm of her hand. "I really wrestled with it for the past couple days, and then this morning it hit me. Thomas was a two-different-shoe kind of person."

She paused.

There were a lot of puzzled looks in the audience, including mine. *What the hell does that mean?*

"When I arrived here this morning I noticed I was wearing two different shoes." Pamela pointed down and lifted one foot out from behind the podium and then the other to model them for the audience. Sure enough, she was wearing a red stiletto and a black stiletto with a little flower over the toes, two totally different shoes. She plowed on, "I was so nervous about doing the service for such an important person in our community that I didn't even notice I was putting on two different shoes this morning. When I got here and noticed, it was too late for me to run home and get the right shoes. I was stuck here with the wrong shoes." She raised her hand. "How many people noticed before I said something? Raise your hand."

Not a hand went up.

A smile played on Pamela's face.

"I didn't think so. Once it hit me what I was going to be talking about, I knew nobody was going to notice. I had a story *that* good. Thomas was like that. He knew something about everything and was interested in everything. He could talk to anyone. Just look around this room. He touched everyone in here, and engaged each and every one of you," she said while poking her finger into the audience, "in such a way that you never had reason to look down and see if he was wearing two different shoes." She paused. "Look where that got him. His life was rich in many ways, most importantly friends and family, and I think the attendance today is a testament to that." Pamela shuffled her notes together and stepped down.

Long after we closed the lid and took Thomas to his place of rest, and the reception was over and I went back to help fold up chairs, and after the first blooms started poking through the ground, and the temperature first hit one hundred degrees Fahrenheit did Pamela's words still knock around in my head. Sadly, I have conducted too many burials where it is just the minister and me. The deceased had nobody else on earth. Nobody. And a man who was almost a century old had more people pay their respects at his service than you'll typically see when a high school–aged kid passes.

I decided to take Pamela's challenge and become a two-different-shoe person. We get so adjusted to our little routine and milieu most of us are terrified of trying something new or are simply too lazy to bother doing something for others. I resolved to stop being complacent and to live more like Thomas. I enrolled in adult classes to learn small engine repair, and how to speak Italian, things I had always talked about doing, started volunteering with my church outreach program, and joined the local Lions Club. I've found that by living like Thomas it doesn't matter even if you are wearing different shoes. Nobody will notice.

CHAPTER 16

Are Mr. Smith and Mr. Wesson in Attendance?

Smith and Wesson or a Colt always beats four aces.
—AMERICAN PROVERB

T here are about 12,300 firearms* sold in America every day.

That's a gun sold every seven seconds, or about nine a minute.

Nine guns sold every single minute.

In the time it takes to hum "America the Beautiful" six legal gun sales have been made.

God Bless America!

Guns are so uniquely American. Yes, the Second Amendment in our Bill of Rights guarantees us the right to bear arms, but we seem to have an obsession with firepower. Apple pie and firearms are the American dream... along with the white picket fence, a GMC and Ford in the driveway, and 2.2 kids and all that good stuff. Where else can you go in the world where citizens are guaranteed the right to own and carry firearms? Almost every other country in the world firearm ownership is *heavily* regu-

---

*According to the Bureau of Alcohol, Tobacco, Firearms, and Explosives.

lated by the state. Take for example Great Britain. The Bobbies walking the beat, the thin blue line separating law and order from looting mobs and anarchy, aren't allowed to carry guns! They give those poor guys a badge and a flashlight and send them out to serve and protect. It's almost laughable that I can hop into my car and ride down to Miller's Gun Shop and buy a carbine rifle (that may or may not have the capability of being converted to fully automatic with just a rubber band) if I decide it's a gun-buying-type day. Or, if I want to go a little less legal route, I can head on over to Thirty-First and Pine and buy a Saturday Night Special for a C-note, or at least that's the going price according to the beat cops.

I guess that's why the good ole USA is the undisputed international champion of percentage of gun ownership by its citizens. There are about 310 million citizens and (depending on whose data you look at) 250 to 300 million guns.* That's almost a gun per citizen! I guess it really isn't that surprising there are that many gun owners. Less than 1 percent of background checks end up denying someone gun ownership. But in reality not every man, woman, and child is toting a gat—only roughly 40 percent of households have firearms.† Obviously, some citizens are buying more guns than they have hands to shoot with. Being white, male, and Republican almost statistically guarantees that I own a gun . . . or four.

But what do guns have to do with funeral directors or funerals? Good question. Nothing, or so I used to think, until I heard these stories. Of course there is the occasional, nonsensical

---

*justfacts.com's data states that in 2009 (when the population was 307 million) there were 300 million firearms.
†According to a 2005 Gallup Nationwide Poll.

drive-by shooting at a funeral—usually gang related—that makes the news, but there is nothing interesting, surprising, or palatable about such travesties. These stories are fascinating because it is the *last* person you'd imagine to have a gun at a funeral is the one packing. But with forty states being "shall issue" states, meaning all you need is a pulse to get a concealed weapon permit, it really isn't surprising there are people packing heat at funerals. Ken and I both live in "may issue" states, which means you have to have a reason to carry concealed. As a result, neither of us sees too many weapons on a daily basis.

Double Duty
Contributed by a writer

For a time I worked for a livery service in Louisiana. Most of the time I drove limousines, but on occasion I drove hearses. Some funeral homes that don't do a large death call volume find it cheaper to simply rent a hearse for the day of a funeral rather than pay a note on it all year. Renting has the upside in that it looks as if that particular funeral home always has the latest and greatest hearse, which is important because the hearse is the most visible aspect of your company. It's always parked outside the church, visible to all those who enter; it's a billboard on wheels.

On a hot July day I was scheduled to do a hearse job for Perkins Mortuary. The drive to the mortuary's chapel was some forty-five minutes out of Lafayette, and though I had taken a cold shower that morning by the time I arrived I was covered in a sheen of sweat despite the best efforts by the air conditioner. I found out when I moved to this state some ten years ago that the word *hot* takes a whole new meaning in Louisiana. It's not a nice dry heat like Nevada; no, it's a sweaty, sticky, pervasive heat that grips a person like an invisible fist and squeezes. Really, the humidity is a good reason not to live in Louisiana.

I had never driven for this particular mortuary before, so I introduced myself to a large, sweaty man who appeared to be in charge. He was. He identified himself as Bobby Perkins. Bobby doesn't really dress "the part" of a funeral director, or at least the ones I'm accustomed to dealing with. Bobby was wearing what appeared to be a zoot suit—white with a black shirt and white tie—that was altogether too small for his enormous frame and he fairly exploded out of it. The padded shoulders of the suit jacket made him appear even larger. Bobby had the noticeable habit of removing a handkerchief from his inner pocket and constantly wiping his face. I wasn't sure if it were a nervous tic or the fact that his face happened to be perpetually red and dripping sweat.

Despite his unusual appearance, he seemed to be very jolly and showed me the employee lounge that was actually a dimly lit grimy kitchenette. He told me to make myself comfortable and disappeared. I sat and ate (what tasted to be) a day-old doughnut and read the newspaper but was scared of the coffee. The pot looked like something from one of the Gemini class space flights.

After a spell I wandered into the lobby. The service was underway. It was for a young man, mid-forties. Typical for the service of a young man, it went on forever and it was packed, standing room only. After the service Bobby went up and made his announcement. I couldn't really understand it because of his accent, but I think it was some sort of dismissal interspersed with a lot of face wiping. The people in the chapel seemed to understand his message because they began to file out.

The pallbearers loaded the casket and Bobby donned a white fedora with a little feather pinned to it and climbed into the hearse with me. The coach listed to the passenger side considerably.

"Let's go," he instructed.

I began to lead the procession.

"Where you from?" he asked. In his heavy Cajun accent it came out more like, "wer' yoo fro'?" But imagine him singing it to me. Cajuns have a very singsong way of talking.

"Uh," I paused, mentally translating. "Florida."

He nodded. "Joie de vivre," he said, then wiped his face and smiled. "Sunshi' sta—"

I had no idea what he said but nodded agreement. Cajuns will sometimes intersperse French into their speech to *really* confuse the untrained listener. Even though I had been in the state ten years I still considered myself untrained. It must take a lifetime to learn the language.

He liked that I agreed, wiped his face, and thus it went: us conversing, me trying to translate, and him occasionally pointing left or right, fanning himself with his hat and mopping his face with his sopping handkerchief. We drove and drove and drove for miles along narrow country roads back in the swamps. Finally, Bobby pointed right and I turned into a tiny churchyard. The church was an ancient-looking white clapboard structure surrounded by lichen-covered headstones.

Bobby pointed to a mound of dirt near the rear of the churchyard and I directed the hearse over near the grave. When we got out Bobby said, "Jo, I wan' you to gaur' the gra-ho. Goin' to be chillin' run' arou'."

Which I took to mean: "Joan, I want you to guard the grave hole. There are going to be children running around."

"Sure," I said. I assumed a position near the giant hole cut in the earth, ready to block any of the dozen children already cut loose from their vehicles and running wild in the graveyard. They didn't make a move for my position, and I soon grew bored and began studying the headstones around me. Time and black lichen had rendered most of them unreadable, save for a few skulls and crossbones still visible.

Bobby rounded up the pallbearers and with much gesticulating and shouting got them to carry the casket over and place it on the worn two-by-four boards laid across the hole. More shouting, this time at the mob, got them to go gather around the somber scene under the towering cypresses where the bespectacled preacher spoke of hellfire and brimstone and the virtues of the Lord. The Bible verses flew through the air, more numerous than the mosquitoes. There were a lot of exclamations of "Amen!" from the crowd, and with a wave of his hat and some more shouting, Bobby dismissed the crowd.

There was a lot more lingering than most burials because of the man's age, but one by one the cars left the church lot until it was just Bobby, the preacher, and me. The preacher was a little dour-faced man, thin as a rail with a fringe of hair running around his otherwise bald head. He was dressed in all black save his lizard-skin cowboy boots. So there I stood with the big white bear and the little black willow listening to the swamp creatures. I knew something was going to happen because Bobby just stood there kicking at the mound of raw earth like he knew what was going to happen next. Soon enough it did, a white panel van slowly navigated down the road toward us. That's when the preacher went to his pickup truck and got a shotgun out. He pumped the action. *Shick, shick.*

"Hey-oh! Hey-oh! Hey-oh!" He began shouting at the van and waving his gun menacingly.

Oh Lord, the preacher has a gun!

I ran over to Bobby, who wasn't paying attention to the scene unfolding. "He's got a gun!" I tried to whisper, but damn near shouted in his ear.

"Huh?"

"Look! Look!" I whisper-shouted. "The preacher. He's got a gun!"

Bobby turned to look at the preacher and the van. He seemed unperturbed. "So?"

"But, but," I spluttered, "he's got a gun!" I was pointing crazily like he couldn't see.

"Me too," Bobby said and reached into his waistband and whipped out a giant shiny revolver.

I nearly fainted. Here I am, alone, in the middle of nowhere with a minister and funeral director both wielding guns, and the minister has his leveled at the approaching van, clearly agitated.

Was there going to be some kind of showdown at the O.K. Corral? I sure as hell wasn't going to stick around and find out. I was heading into the swamp. I'd take my chances with the gators.

My distress with the situation must've finally registered with him because he hastily stowed his gun and made a calming motion with his hands. "It's okay," he said. "The preacher is also the deputy sheriff."

I looked again and the preacher wasn't pointing his shotgun at the van, but using it as a pointer to motion the driver where to go. The van bumped to a stop and orange-clad men piled out with LDOC stamped on their backs. Prisoners.

Now the preacher was pointing the weapon. He pointed and shouted. The prisoners didn't acknowledge his presence, but it appeared as if they had been through this drill before. They retrieved two giant coils of rope from the van and ran them under the casket. A man got on each end of the two pieces of rope and a fifth prisoner pulled the boards out from under the casket. With a lot of grunting from the prisoners and cussing and shouting from the preacher the men lowered the casket into the hole. They exchanged rope for shovels and began to fill the hole in. It was unbearably hot just standing watching them, so I can't imagine how miserable it must've been for them.

On the way back I asked Bobby, "Do you always carry a gun?"

He smiled and fanned himself with his hat. "Everyone in Louisiana owns a gun, even preachers. But I don't make a practice of carrying mine to burials except when there are going to be convicts there." He wiped his face and winked at me.

The Terrorist
Contributed by a vinyl collector

The pundits claim that in order for an attack to be defined as "terroristic" it has to have political motivation. I disagree. I witnessed an attack at a funeral without any such attached political agenda but it still struck terror into the hearts of all in attendance as evidenced by the ensuing pandemonium. The attack came out of nowhere, and with no forewarning as terrorist attacks tend to, and it all happened one fine September day.

I was the first one in on the day of the attack. I'm always first in. I think it was my days in the military that make me such an early riser. My body has an internal alarm clock. Bam, 4:30, I'm wide awake. I take a leisurely jog, make my first pot of coffee of the day, surf the Internet, and am at work hours before anyone else. On this particular day my daughter was having a father-daughter doughnut day at her elementary school, so I arrived only a few minutes before everyone else.

As I wheeled around the building, I cursed out loud—some choice words I'd learned in the military. There, lying next to the building, were the flowers for Mr. York's funeral. Intolerable. For a number of reasons we tell florists *never* to leave the flowers outside, one of them being this time of year can get particularly hot in this region of the country and turn a nice arrangement into a wilted mess. Thankfully it was still early, and the temperature temperate.

I palmed the wheel into my parking space (we don't have assigned spots, but since I'm always first I have my pick) and collected the newspaper. I set coffee to brew as I unlocked the building for the day's festivities. It's almost a prerequisite for being a funeral director that you guzzle coffee by the gallon. In fact, I think that's a question on the entrance exam to all mortuary colleges: *Do you drink coffee? If you answered no, are you willing to start?* But even after years in the military and current profession, I hate regular coffee. So I drink hazelnut, vanilla in a pinch. Some say flavored coffee isn't coffee at all; I argue that's splitting hairs. Least it's not lattes.

Used to be, when I started, the prerequisite was cigarettes *and* coffee, but these days of smoking bans, even in Phillip Morris country, the new recruits don't smoke. I only have two colleagues left who are walking smokestacks. The breed is changing; hazelnut coffee drinking, nonsmoking undertakers are taking over.

I poured a cup of hazelnut into my mug, still unwashed from yesterday, left it too cool, and unlocked the door to the flower room. We lock it at night. No sense inviting trouble. When I swung open the door, the sight of stupidity caused me to unleash another sailor's string of language. All the florists know when we open. It's not my problem if one of your deliveries doesn't fit into my schedule. I made a mental note to call the florist later and give them a dressing down.

I didn't even need to read the little card stuck in the plastic stick to know these arrangements were from Blooms.

Believe it or not, all florists have a signature for how they arrange. I can look at any arrangement that comes through the door and immediately tell which florist it's from. Common sense would dictate that flowers are flowers are flowers, but that's not the case. Different florists use different qualities and quantities of flowers in their arrangements and the way the flowers are arranged in a particular piece, even the vase or basket, contributes to an individual florist's signature.

Blooms is known for their gigantic casket sprays. This was no exception. To say the thing was huge would be an understatement. It was *massive*. I hefted the spray up and grunted. The damn thing weighed a ton. I carried it as fast as I could into the viewing room without stabbing myself in the eye with a protruding stick. The floral designer at Blooms had decided on a fall mixture that included twigs and leaves and mums and all sorts stuff that made it kind of look like a compost pile. I hung the enormous horn of plenty on Mr. York's casket. The lid teetered from the weight but held. As a safety precaution I took a bit of baling wire and wired the cornucopia to the rack holding it on the lid. I didn't want this albatross falling on some little old lady's head as she bent to kiss Mr. York.

I retrieved the matching baskets and set them up around the casket, all the while muttering about how I could've raked something better together in my yard, and then went to find my coffee.

The family arrived in a stretch limo and soon guests began arriving to pay their respects to the York family. I stood in the lobby and did my usual thing of inviting guests to sign the guest registry and then handing them a memorial folder. Mr. and Mrs. York live in a retirement/assisted living facility, as such most of the place turned out. There were a lot of walkers, canes, and wheelchairs. But you find that a lot these days with everyone living longer and all that. The assisted living facility even sent their little bus over to drop off a load of residents who couldn't drive anymore, and with Mr. York's children's friends the room was packed by the time the boyish-faced Lutheran pastor stepped to the lectern, ready to begin.

He nodded to me.

I stepped forward.

It is part of the Christian tradition to have the casket closed during the service so the people of the congregation can focus on worship, not the body. That being said, a lot of ministers will bow to the family's wishes in a funeral home setting and leave it open. So don't think it's the law to have a casket closed during a Christian service, just tradition.

"Ladies and gentleman," I said from my position at the lectern, "in keeping with the Christian tradition of worship, we will at this time close the casket. Anyone uncomfortable with this, please step to the lobby and I'll come get you before the service." I made a sweeping gesture with my arm toward the lobby.

A couple of old women got up and shuffled off.

I motioned again with my arm, this time a smaller gesture to Mr. York's children and grandchildren. They knew what I was motioning them to do. We had discussed it during the funeral arrangements conference and again when they arrived. It was time for them to say good-bye.

One by one they came up with their respective families and said their tearful good-byes: son, daughter, and son.

When they were done I helped Mrs. York up and escorted her to the casket.

I discretely stepped aside while she laid her hands on the face of her husband of sixty-one years and wept. She put her head down near his shoulder as if to whisper something and that's when the terrorist made his move.

He poked his head up out of the casket spray and looked side to side. I only caught movement out of the corner of my eye and before I could react he hopped down from the spray onto the blanket.

Mrs. York's head snapped up and she screamed when she saw the squirrel standing stock still, tail straight up, on the blanket at her husband's legs.

Her scream scared the big fat squirrel and he hopped up onto the edge of the casket, took stock of his audience, and leaped off the casket and ran down the aisle at a brisk clip.

The place erupted in pandemonium.

Mrs. York continued screaming, leaped back, catching her foot on the casket stand. Thankfully I was right behind her to catch her as she went down. She stopped mid-scream and fainted. I laid her gently on the floor and stood to assess the riot. "Calm down! Calm down!" I shouted. But there was no calming this crowd.

People using wheelchairs and canes were fighting their way toward the lobby. I saw one old woman who had tottered in on a walker throw the walker aside, body check another old woman out of the way, and sprint toward the exit. It looked almost like a European football brawl if it took place in a nursing home.

I spied the squirrel climbing some drapes in the back of the room. It reached the top and disappeared behind the jabot. Realizing that quelling the riot wasn't an option, I raced over to the door we take the casket out and threw it open. I had a plan to herd the squirrel outside and thus quiet the riot by getting rid of the terrorist.

The lobby was packed. There was no way I was pushing through that mob to get a broom. The only option was a microphone stand.

"What do we do with mother?" Sam York yelled, kneeling on the floor, cradling his mother's head in his lap.

I dropped the mic stand. "Let's get her to the sofa in the lobby. Tim," I said to Sam's brother, "give us a hand here." The three of us lifted the unconscious form of Mrs. York and carried her out to the lobby where the patrons were milling liked spooked cattle. "Clear the way!" I called in my best all-hands-on-deck voice, plowing through the sea of geriatric humanity until we reached the sofa. I piled two throw pillows under Mrs. York's ankles in an effort to get her feet above her heart.

"Tim," I commanded, "go to the bathroom and soak a towel in cold water and apply it to her forehead, and Sam, you get her a drink of water."

I didn't wait for them to move before I was running back toward the service room.

I found the pastor alone in the room. "I've got a gun in my car," he said.

I guess my quick look prompted him to add, "I hunt a lot. It's a little .22 rifle I'm teaching my son on that I think I could get him with."

I'm a conservative, but even I don't condone the execution of a terrorist without a trial—that and I didn't want to wash squirrel blood out of the draperies.

"Get him?"

"Yeah," he said. "Shoot him."

I didn't really need him to clarify, I knew what he had meant by "get him." "No," I said. "We're not shooting off guns in here."

"I'm a good shot."

"No."

"Marksman Second Class at my range," he persisted.

"No!"

"Suit yourself," he replied and shrugged.

I grabbed the mic stand, approached the drapes, and prodded them. Nothing. I prodded harder and began to hit them. Still nothing. I figured the squirrel must've fled the scene when I was in the lobby so I lifted the corner of the drape and peeked.

The squirrel came flying by my head at about a hundred miles an hour. I screamed like a girl, dropped the mic stand, and fell backward.

The spectator pastor, stoic against the wall, laughed.

I stood, brushing myself off, feeling foolish, only to watch the squirrel disappearing into another set of drapes on the other side of the room.

I picked up my trusty prodding rod, took a deep breath, and approached the drapes.

Back and forth we went across the room with no herding being accomplished.

At one point Sam poked his head in to ask, "Is he gone?" only to emit a little scream and slam the door as a gray bullet darted by him.

I was growing weary of the game when the squirrel made an error in judgment: instead of climbing the drapes, it hopped onto the rim of the casket and back into the floral spray it rode in on.

I swiped a considerable amount of sweat off my brow. "Do you have a penknife?" I whispered loudly to the pastor, not wanting to disturb the beast.

He nodded and produced one.

I took it from him and tiptoed behind the casket and cut the wire holding it to the rack. Ever so slowly I lifted the spray from where it lay and, carrying it as far away from my body as possible, carried it to the open doors and flung it into the side yard like it was on fire.

Closing the doors to the viewing room, I noticed the drapes were in tatters and smeared with feces. *Small price to pay to winning the war on terror,* I mused sardonically. Flinging the doors to the lobby open, I announced, "Ladies and Gentleman the terror level is now green." Just kidding, I didn't say that. I said something a lot less glib like, "The squirrel has been chased outside. The service for Mr. York will now begin."

As the guests shuffled back into the viewing room, I noted many of them had seemed spryer on the way out.

CHAPTER 17

Ouija

My religion consists of humble admiration of the illimitable superior spirit who reveals himself in the slight details we are able to perceive with our frail and feeble mind.

—ALBERT EINSTEIN

April a few years ago I had some friends over for a seemingly forgettable evening. Recently something happened to bring that night screaming back with the weight of a freight train plowing through my living room. The night of my seemingly forgettable evening, my guests thought it'd be a lark to bring an Ouija board to my dinner party. After all, their friend is a funeral director, he should be a medium to the afterlife, or so must've been their thought process.

We had a dinner of grilled tri-tip—a California delicacy. I'm a pretty bad cook, but I can muddle through with a simple meal on the grill. I bought the sides and dessert at the market and took credit for making them. After dinner we sat in the living room with the scent of the budding orange and peach trees wafting through the open windows and drank coffee and gossiped. It was then that Lacey whipped out the Ouija Board.

"Look what I brought over to play," she said, shaking the box suggestively with a big, silly grin plastered on her face.

"Oh, Christ," I said. "Isn't that thing for junior high kids at sleepovers trying to scare the crap out of each other?"

"What?" she said in a goading voice. "Are you scared of what it'll reveal?"

Not taking the bait, I said, "Please."

"Come on, Ken," Steve said. "It'll be fun." As an afterthought, or a shot at me, he added, "I don't think I've seen one of these things since junior high."

I gave in because I didn't have a better suggestion and we tinkered around with it for an hour before I became irate with Lacey for cheating. The "information" we got from her cheating was that a woman had died in my house during the month of May and she hated men.

"Hated men?" It was her way of pranking me. A man-hating ghost living in a gay man's house? Come on! I declared my boredom with the game and suggested we go for a swim in the pool.

Recently I was doing yard work in the front yard when a voice behind me said, "Excuse me." I dropped the bag of gravel I was carrying and turned to see a neatly dressed woman who was probably in her late fifties standing on the sidewalk. She was wearing a summer dress with a colorful pattern on it. Behind her was an idling car with another woman peering out. The woman on the sidewalk wasn't one of my neighbors, and the first thought that popped into my head was: *this must be a family member of someone I've buried.* This happens frequently, getting stopped by family members of someone I've buried in the past. I like to think I have a pretty good memory, but I can't remember every single family member of the thousands of people I've buried over the years. But I still racked my brain trying to place her. I drew a blank.

"Hi," I said, "can I help you with something?" I smiled and took off my canvas gloves and wiped my brow.

"Do you know who owns this house?" she inquired, obviously thinking I was the gardener.

"I do," I replied.

"Oh," she said, seeming embarrassed.

"Why?"

"It's just that my great-grandmother used to own this house. My sister and I"—she gestured toward the car—"are in town visiting my mother and thought we'd take a drive to see if we could find her place." She smoothed her hands on her dress. "God, it looks just like I remember it. I was worried I wouldn't recognize it. It's been years since I've been here."

"Been out of town long?"

"Yeah," she said, not really hearing what I was saying. Staring at the house, she said, almost to herself, "So many good memories here."

I figured she was fishing for an invitation. I was game, so I said, "Want to take a look around?"

The woman nodded enthusiastically. "That would be great!" She motioned for her sister.

I introduced myself and the woman introduced herself as Mindy and the sister exiting the car as Cindy.

"We're also trying to figure out where she's buried," Mindy said. "Since we're in town. We figured we'd visit her grave."

"When did she die?" I asked.

The sisters argued for a minute before deciding on 1951.

"The old Sunnyside over at Willow and Orange," I said without hesitation. "Ask for Mike. He'll help you locate the grave."

They stared at me with the most peculiar look and it took me a moment to realize a complete stranger had just told them where their great-grandmother was buried. They must've thought I was clairvoyant.

I laughed at their confusion, and said to clear up their mystery, "No, I'm not a psychic. I own a mortuary. If she died during that era there's a very good chance that's the cemetery she's in."

We all got a good laugh out of their surprise and then I took them on a tour; or I should more aptly say they gave me a history lesson. All the land around my house at one time had been a giant parcel with a citrus grove on it. Their great-grandmother had inherited the land, and built the house in 1912. I showed them how I had restored all the woodwork and tilework in the house, and modernized it while maintaining the character of the historic home. "It looks just like I remember," they kept saying as we walked around the house.

When we got to the top of the stairs Cindy pointed to the right, where my room is, and said, "That's the room Oma died in."

The irony of that statement wasn't lost on me.

The sisters had been awfully young when Oma died, but remembered her bed pushed under the window to catch the ocean breeze and so she could smell the trees.

"She simply loved the smell of the orange trees," Mindy said.

All of the sudden, I don't know what came over me, or why I remembered, but I asked, "Did she die in May?"

They stopped prattling on about the trees and looked at me with *that* look they had had earlier. "What did you say?" Cindy asked.

"Did she die in the month of May?"

They had the most peculiar expressions on their faces. "No," Cindy said slowly. "That was her name."

It was my turn to be surprised. "Her *name*? M-a-y?"

"M-a-e," Cindy said. "Her real name was Mabel. It's who I was named after, but everyone in the family called her Mae, kind of like everyone calls me by my middle name, Cindy."

"Eerie," I said.

"Why did you ask that?" Cindy said.

I proceeded to tell them about the Ouija game several years prior including the piece about how she hated men.

Mindy laughed and playfully hit her sister. "Oh my God!" They exchanged knowing looks. I stood there like a bump on a log hoping they would clue me in. "Mae actually loved men," Mindy said. "She was married three times. In fact she's buried next to the first two of them in the Sunnyside, if in fact that's where they are. But her third husband was a farmhand. He was younger than her, and the family suspects he only married her for her money. At the time of their divorce it was the biggest divorce payout in the county's history from a woman to a man. She became a little embittered after that."

"She never quite got over it," Cindy said. "After the divorce, she lived alone for the rest of her life. Never wanted to fool with another man."

"Wow," I said, clapping my hands at the absurdity of what I was hearing. The game had been eerily correct, and here I thought Lacey had just been fooling around. And I know for a fact it wasn't some drunken conjured-up memory like dinner parties of yore used to be for me. I have been winning the battle with the bottle for the past few years, and prefer not to have people drink in my house. I know we were all stone sober when we played.

Since Mindy and Cindy's visit, I have visited Mae's grave and placed some freshly picked oranges on it.

CHAPTER 18

After [Death]

From my rotting body, flowers shall grow and I am in them and that is eternity.

—EDVARD MUNCH

K en and I got a lot of feedback on *MC:USTD*. Mostly they were clarification questions, like, "Do you really do that?" or "Is that what you would do if—" They weren't all questions. Some of the feedback was in regard to something I made mention of earlier, people wanting to share their experiences with death. The one piece of feedback that constantly comes up, and I am still surprised by, goes something like this: "Hey Todd, I really enjoyed the book...until the last chapter when it just got absurd and unrealistic." The last chapter of *MC:USTD*, titled "Thaliea," has to do with the supernatural. Ken and I thought it would be a nice way to round out the book by ending on an ambiguous subject that is really the biggie, *what happens when we die?*

I didn't realize it would generate such disbelief.

So, when gathering ideas for this book, Ken and I specifically set out to gather some more material dealing with the spirit world and afterlife. And find it we did. A woman I work closely with who is a certified funeral celebrant and grief counselor, Dr.

Rosemary Castelli, approached me and said, "Todd, I have a story to tell you about the subject matter you're interested in, but you might not believe me."

Try me.

She proceeded to tell me a story so fantastic and freaky it sounded like the script for a Wes Craven movie. In fact, once I put it together and edited it down, I was told by various literary authorities we were plying this project on that, "it wasn't within the scope of the work."

True, it was a little removed from funeral homes and undertakers, but it was a gem of a story. Long story short, Rosie—what everyone calls her—ran a bed and breakfast that was inhabited by several spirits who would "interact" with the guests. And when a medium came to the house, she determined that the business office had a cold presence and she felt the presence of multiple dead people in the basement. Upon further investigation Rosie found out the house had been a funeral parlor. The office had a cold "presence" because it used to be the cold storage room (what we would now call a walk-in refrigerator) and the basement had been the embalming room.

Hearing Rosie talk about her experiences in this house, she almost didn't believe what she was telling me, or was afraid that I'd be skeptical of what she was telling me. In her professional life, she was a vice president for a college. She *was* the type of person to not believe . . . until she retired and bought a B&B. But I'm a believer. I was born in a house with a spirit presence. Rosie need not preach to me; I'm the choir.

I've come to the conclusion there are two types of people in this world: believers and nonbelievers. Really, the only thing that separates the two is experience. As a rational human being I'd like to think I wouldn't believe either, but I also know as a rational human being, science hasn't unlocked every secret in the universe yet. We haven't even begun to scratch the surface, so I am open to new, reasonable ideas.

Of course this subject isn't very reasonable. It's strictly visceral.

If you're a nonbeliever, and unwilling to suspend disbelief to at least get through the end of the book, stop here. This is the end of the book for you. Seriously, close the book because anything after this will just upset you.

But, if you're a believer, or someone with an open mind, then, I urge you: give it a chance. My college roommate is, perhaps, one of the most skeptical people I know. If I told him the sky was blue, he'd want to go out and check before agreeing, but more than likely, he'd argue the point that it was more sapphire than true blue. He grew up in a three-hundred-year-old house that's as haunted as Elvis is dead. He won't sleep there alone, that's how bad it is. So, if he unequivocally believes in the metaphysical world, I don't feel so crazy either.

But even those nonbelievers are curious. I seem to get asked, "Are there ghosts at the funeral home?" I don't really have the faintest idea—other than pure speculation—about what happens spiritually or otherwise after death, but it seems the spirit likes to inhabit the place it lived, or died, or a place that had some other special significance in its life . . . not the building where its earthly remains were given last rites. That being said, my uncle is probably going to haunt the funeral home one day.

This final story isn't so much a ghost story as it is one mortician's affirmation that death isn't the end, merely a stage.

Through the Curtains
Contributed by a gym rat

I don't pretend to understand the machinations of the universe; I'm just a humble mortician. I care for the mortal remains, the soul's tabernacle, and let God figure out all the rest. Over the years I've faced hundreds of different people across my desk and listened to them recount the gritty details of their loved one's death. And while every death is unique, I've come to believe from these stories, which have a reoccurring theme, that there is *something* more than our world.

Death is not an inorganic moment of nothingness, as one may believe, but a piece in the puzzle of the time-space continuum. For many years this was just anecdotal evidence I collected across my desk. I was a believer, but I had no real evidence of my own. That is, until my grandma died.

Grandma's illness was my first firsthand familial experience with hospice. Generally, I ride in on the coattails of hospice; the hospice nurse's final act is to hand the pronunciation of death to me, shake the family's hands, and leave. That is what I see, and that's when my job starts. But I got to see it from its inception when Grandma fell ill in the fall of last year.

I don't know if it has anything to do with the Depression, but people of her generation seem to distrust doctors. Grandma steadfastly refused to see any medical professional unless she was on death's door. She was this way her entire life. By the time they caught it—lung cancer—it had infiltrated her lymph system and had spread everywhere. What had started as a persistent cough morphed so just a couple of months later there was nothing they could do.

"How can I have lung cancer?" she proclaimed, ever

suspicious of the diagnosis until the day of her death. "I never smoked a day in my life!"

Pneumonia hit her as the weather turned cold, and she was hospitalized. The hospital stabilized her, called my mom, and told her it was time for hospice care. Then they sent her home to die. That's what the hospice movement is all about, allowing people to die peacefully and dignified in the comfortable surroundings of their own home. It is really a great program, and a throwback to several generations ago when the medical establishment consisted of country doctors making house calls and our ancestors routinely died at home in their beds surrounded by family members.

It was touch and go for a week. Thankfully, with my job, I can be very flexible, and I was able to spend most of my week at the family house. I have many fond memories growing up of going over to my grandparents' house for holiday meals and special occasions like birthdays and anniversary parties. Most of that week Grandma was on hospice care was spent catching up with out-of-town family, eating take-out food, looking at old photos, and laughing. But the laughter was that kind of bittersweet laughter: funny stories that you are only telling *because* of the occasion. I hear them all the time in eulogies and casual conversation during wakes. My familiarity with that type of grief talk didn't make it any easier to be a part of.

On Thursday night I got a call at eleven o'clock. It was my mom. Grandma probably wouldn't make it through the night. I'm used to late-night calls filled with sorrow, but being around it doesn't prepare you for it. I pulled on my jeans with a heavy heart.

Surprisingly, Grandma made it through the night.

At dawn I left to get coffee and a box of doughnuts. The sun was breaking over the horizon when I cruised back into her neighborhood. She and Grandpa never had that much.

They both worked hard all their lives and made a nice life for themselves and their three children. The neighborhood is one of those that sprang up in the late fifties to accommodate the boomer-era explosion. The houses are on the small side, and packed in together, but the neighbors always maintain them immaculately. The neighborhood was turning over, I noticed. Lots of kiddie bikes and jungle gyms littered the lawns. Hopefully a nice young family with kids would buy Grandma's house. I knew she would want that—another family to make joyful memories in her home.

I pulled my hearse up in front of the saltbox house, painted mint green with white awnings, sighed, and got out. In contrast to the comforting smell of coffee in the leathery confines of the hearse the overpowering smell of dying assaulted my senses as I entered. It was stronger than yesterday. I knew the end was close. Death has a very distinct smell.

My uncles, their wives, my mom, and I, along with a few cousins, squeezed into the cheerful confines of the kitchen to drink coffee and eat doughnuts. It was almost like a holiday: we laughed, and drank, and ate in the ample sunshine afforded by the bay window until Terri, the nurse, appeared in the doorway.

"It's going to be soon," she said gently. I could tell by the look on her face it genuinely pained her to tell us the news.

We filled Grandma's bedside. Her breathing was very erratic. It got slower and more ragged. At one point I thought she was gone, but she drew in a great breath, opened her eyes and spoke for the first time in three days, "There he is! And he has Will!"

She closed her eyes and died.

But in doing so, vindicated my belief in that *something* in the universe.

My mom held one of her gray hands, and turned to look

at me, tears streaming out of her eyes, "Can you believe it?" she asked.

I just smiled and nodded through my own tears.

The "he" who Grandma had referred to was her husband who died three years ago, and Will was William, their son who died sixty years ago.

After we sat quietly in the room for a bit I said, "Okay."

The rest of the family knew what it meant and ushered themselves out. I spent a moment, said a silent prayer, and placed two pennies in Grandma's hand, one with her year of birth and one with her year of death. "That should get you where you need to be," I muttered. The lore behind that little tradition is so the dead can pay the toll to the ferryman, Charon, for a ride across the River Styx to the underworld. In medieval times the pennies were placed on the eyes not only to pay the toll but for the more practical purpose of keeping the eyes closed during the wake. Being a funeral director, I'm prone to a bit of superstition. It can't hurt.

My brother-in-law helped me carry the earthly remains of Grandma down the stairs, and a colleague met me at the mortuary to embalm her. Later that night, lying in bed, I was exhausted, but couldn't sleep. Her last words kept running through my mind and what those words meant.

Before my mom was born, my grandparents' first child, William, died in infancy. Nobody knows how he died, but the general consensus is that it would be what we now know as SIDS, or sudden infant death syndrome. No rhyme. No reason. They woke up one morning and poor Will was gone. Apparently, it devastated Grandma. She *never* spoke of Will ever again. Ever. Her family knew never to even bring up his name in her presence for it upset her so much. Grandpa told it to my mom in his usual trying-to-be-sweet but gruff manner when she was older after she stumbled upon a picture of infant Will in Grandpa's war steamer trunk in the attic. Grandma never even knew about the photo; she destroyed all photos of her firstborn soon after his death. His image, she told Grandpa, was simply too painful too bear. Grandpa, not the sentimental type, hid one photo of his firstborn. That was his way of dealing with his grief. I suspect he would bring the photo out now and then to look at it.

Grandma took the death much harder than her husband. Most people turn to faith during a crisis. Grandma did the opposite; she cast it off after the death of her son. I never asked her, but I suspect her logic was, "How can a God exist that would take a child?" Grandma's father had been an evangelical preacher, a tent revivalist, and growing up she had "followed the rules." When the "rules" failed her, she had abandoned them.

Like I said earlier, Grandma was a product of the Depression. She internalized her feelings and just carried on with a stiff upper lip, doing what needed doing. As a result, nobody ever knew her real reasons about the issue. It is all speculation on my part. These thoughts swirled through my head as I eventually drifted off to sleep.

The next day, I awoke after only a few hours' sleep, surprisingly rested. It was Saturday, but the dead know no days, and the day found me at the mortuary, sitting across the desk from another bereaved person hearing a story I have heard hundreds of time: people die, yes, but they aren't lost in the universe, they are merely moving on. On this particular day, for the first time, I was able to reciprocate my experience, and we sat and grieved together.

William Blake wrote, "If the doors of perception were cleansed every thing would appear to man as it is, infinite." And for a brief moment the curtain parted and Grandma was able to look across infinity, with one foot still in the realm of the living, and let us know everything was going to be all right; her husband was standing with her son, waiting for her arrival.

She stepped through, the curtain closed, and all that was left were us mere mortals.

Acknowledgments

(by Todd)

First, I'd like to express my sincerest gratitude to you, the reader. If there hadn't been such demand generated from *Mortuary Confidential* this book wouldn't exist. Publishing Darwinism: 80 percent of books fail. Ken and I were lucky to skate in with the scant 20 percent because of you.

Second, I'd like to thank Michaela Hamilton, our amazing editor at Kensington, for believing in *Over Our Dead Bodies* and helping us put together an excellent, albeit moribund (sorry, funeral director humor), product.

There were several people during the different incarnations of this work who helped to ultimately shape it to what you're reading. Elana, Caren, Chris, and Caitlin helped in minor and major ways. Also, the many, many people and brethren who have shared their stories; you gave me something to wordsmith.

Scotty Nav, a longtime partner in crime, continues to offer his web design prowess.

Scott and Meg Harra and the other Rakkasans and soldiers who continue to guarantee our First Amendment Rights.

Of course, this book wouldn't exist without Uncle Rick. He has taken me under his wing and taught me the profession from the inside out. I have never met someone who loves what they do for a living more that he does. I give Uncle Rick credit for introducing me to Ken. He spied a little ad in *American Funeral Director* for the calendar and paid my entry fee.

Finally, my family. Being a writer means many solitary hours, and my wife is exceedingly patient with me. For me, it was a strange contrariety laboring over a book about death while welcoming new life into the world.

(by Ken)

I want to thank my co-author, Todd, for taking the lead on this project when I found myself consumed with personal losses.

Also, I want to acknowledge the thousands of families I have served the past twenty-seven years. *Thank you.* I am eternally grateful that you entrusted the care of your loved ones to me.

Your purchase of *Over Our Dead Bodies* is helping women who are battling breast cancer. A portion of the proceeds of this book is being donated to the KAMM Cares Foundation. For more information or to make a donation, please visit www.kammcares.org.

KAMM CARES
Cancer Foundation
"Coping through comfort."
Founded December 2005
www.KammCares.org

Connect with U(s)

Visit us online at
KensingtonBooks.com
to read more from your favorite authors, see books
by series, view reading group guides, and more.

Join us on social media

for sneak peeks, chances to win books and prize packs,
and to share your thoughts with other readers.

facebook.com/kensingtonpublishing
twitter.com/kensingtonbooks

Tell us what you think!

To share your thoughts, submit a review,
or sign up for our eNewsletters, please visit:
KensingtonBooks.com/TellUs.